# COOKING
## with
# BEER

## Taste-Tempting Recipes and Creative Ideas for Matching Beer & Food

## LUCY SAUNDERS

TIME® LIFE BOOKS

TIME-LIFE BOOKS, ALEXANDRIA, VIRGINIA
PRINTED IN CANADA

TIME-LIFE BOOKS IS A DIVISION OF TIME LIFE INC.


TIME LIFE CUSTOM PUBLISHING

Vice President and Publisher — Terry Newell
Managing Editor — Donia Ann Steele
Director of New Product Development — Regina Hall
Director of Sales — Neil Levin
Director of Special Sales — Liz Ziehl
Director of Rights and Licensing — Teresa Hartnett

First Printing. Printed in Canada.
Published simultaneously in Canada.

TIME-LIFE is a trademark of Time Warner Inc. U.S.A.

Produced by Storey Communications, Inc.,
105 Schoolhouse Road, Pownal, Vermont 05261

President — M. John Storey
Executive Vice President — Martha M. Storey
Vice President and Publisher — Pamela B. Art
Custom Publishing Director — Amanda R. Haar
Editors — Amanda R. Haar, Deirdre Lynch, and Angela Cardinali
Cover and Text Design — Black Trout Design, Carol J. Jessop
Text Production — Black Trout Design, Faith E. Kaufman
Illustrations — Laura Tedeschi

Library of Congress Cataloging-in-Publication Data

Saunders, Lucy.
    Cooking with beer : taste-tempting recipes and creative ideas
for matching beer & food / [by Lucy Saunders].
        p.      cm.
    Includes index.
    ISBN 0-7835-4832-X
    1. Cookery (Beer)   2. Beer.   I. Time-Life Books.   II.
Title.
    TX726.3.S28     1996
    641.6'23—dc20

                                        96-15720
                                        CIP

# DEDICATION

*To my grandmother, Phyllis Woodruff,*
*whose love has blessed four generations*

# TABLE OF CONTENTS

# ACKNOWLEDGMENTS

Though experience alone is a great teacher, any skill is learned so much more quickly when knowledge is shared. The following people have generously shared their time, resources, knowledge, and encouragement (plus many pints of beer) over the years. In alphabetical order, I thank:

Stephen Baker, Karen Barker, Larry Baush, Steve Beaumont, Tom Bedell, Liz Branch, Marietta Abrams Brill, Bob Bonsberg, Dan Bradford, Deborah and Dan Carey, Peter Coulson, Sally Cruikshank, Tom Dalldorf, Michael Davis, Roger Deschner, Jennifer Dinehart, Keith Dinehart, Fred Dodsworth, Sara Doersam, Mark Dorber, Frank Doucette, Dave Edgar, Charles Finkel, Linda Funk, David Furer, Patrick Geoghegan, Seth Gross, Carol Guensburg, Erik Gunn, Amanda Haar, Bob Hafenbrack, Rob Haiber, Steve Hamburg, John Hansell, Regi Heise, Mike Hennick, John Hickenlooper, Michael Horne, Michael Jackson, Steve and Danielle Johnson, Steve Joseph, Marc Kadish, Chris Kenneally, Jack Kenny, Russ and May Klisch, Debra Koller, Daria Labinsky, Paula Lambert, Barbara Lang, Wendy Littlefield, Iain Loe, Rick Lyke, Ann Maedke, Mark May, Molly McQuade, Nancy Moore, Randy Mosher, Benjamin Myers, Sue Nowak, Bill Owens, Christa Percival, Rupert Ponsonby, Jill Prescott, Jean Paul Rodriguez, Fred Rosen, Bob Schaffer, Candy Schermerhorn, Arthur Seddon, Ilse Shelton, Nick Sholley, Bill Siebel, Mark Silva, Billy Simms, Alan Skversky, Gregg Smith, Randy Sprecher, Donia Steele, Nancy Stohs, Erin Vang and Pamela and Jonathan Zearfoss.

Love to Tom, Bill and Sally, Margery and Tony, and the Balding, Budd, Carter, Geilfuss, Miller, Pierce, Piper, Saunders, Theis, and Woodruff families.

# CHAPTER 1

# FLAVOR FIRST

## ABOUT BEER AT AMERICA'S TABLE

Beer is humanity's earliest and most enduring choice of refreshment, an elixir of grain and water transformed by yeast and hops. Ancient brews made by tribes and villages have evolved into a global brewing industry with hundreds of "new" brands introduced each year. In drinking and cooking with today's new brews, modern Americans really are rediscovering the variety in styles and depths of flavor that are possible in beer—a variety that other cultures around the world have been enjoying for centuries.

At America's table, beer can be both a favored companion to food and a superb cooking ingredient. The monopoly that light lager has long held in the American market is giving way to a huge variety of styles. A world of new tastes awaits the cook who is just beginning to explore the realm of craft beers (also known as "microbrews").

Actually, craft beers may be brewed by both small microbreweries and larger breweries. To be called a "microbrewery," the brewery must produce fewer than 15,000 barrels of beer per year. Yet there are many breweries whose production volume is too large for the "microbrew" label, but whose quality remains "hand-crafted" (Catamount, Sierra Nevada, August Schell, and Leinenkugels, to name just a few). Such brews typically are made entirely from grain (not malt extracts, grits, or corn syrups) and specialty hops in a wide spectrum of flavorful beer styles.

Some of the new craft beers actually are brewed from old recipes. Since beer's origins date from the beginning of civilization, there are plenty of ancient texts to inspire brewers. According to Alan Eames, beer historian, one of the oldest cuneiform tablets from the Tigris-Euphrates region boasted that Ebla beer "has the heart of a lion."

Not only have advertisements been translated, but so have formulas for brewing beer. Anchor Brewing Co. recreated an ancient Sumerian recipe for beer and named it Ninkasi after the goddess of brewing arts. Though Ninkasi was a one-time experiment, there are several historic styles of beer now available on the market. These include a porter brewed from a recipe recently discovered in an 18th century London text, an ale brewed according to tasting notes by Thomas Hardy, the English novelist and poet, and a Norse ale brewed from a recipe handbook dating back to the 17th century.

Beer was called "liquid bread" in the monasteries of medieval Europe where it was consumed for nutrition during Lenten fasts, and for good health (to brew good beer, water must be boiled and sanitary). Across Europe, until well into the 19th century, women were the primary brewers; they not only baked bread, but also brewed "small" beer using the basic ingredients of grain, yeast, and water, augmented by hops or spices. Even today, in parts of Latin America, Asia, and Africa women often are the chief brewers.

Now, as the 21st century approaches, North America's boom in craft beer mirrors the rise of specialty baking. We can choose from hand-shaped loaves of mouthwatering variety: crusty French sourdough, caraway-studded rye, dark pumpernickel, rustic round breads flavored with grated cheeses or flecked with fresh rosemary, chewy bagels, tender pita pockets, and more. With such a wide selection of breads to choose from, why limit ourselves to forever eating plain sliced white bread? Similarly, why limit ourselves to North American light lager when there are so many other delicious styles available?

But just like the popularity of sliced white bread, there are more factors than mere flavor that make American light lager such a popular choice. Price, economies of scale due to mass production, distribution, advertising, and other influences shape our tastes. Historic and economic shifts have also contributed to the changes in flavors and styles of American beer. Prohibition closed many breweries forever. For the few surviving breweries, World War II represented another challenge as imported barley malts were scarce, along with gasoline, glass, and other resources. Brewers then discovered that it was possible to brew light lager more cheaply through the use of adjuncts, such as domestically grown corn. By the 1950s, advertising showed light lager as the most refreshing and affordable style of beer. Consumers quickly became accustomed to paying low prices for light style beer (hence the popular phrase, "living on a beer budget").

American light lagers still are heavily promoted as simple thirst quenchers for adults, and not often advertised as accompaniments to food. But thousands of curious drinkers, drawn by the seasonal and specialty craft beers, now look beyond the labels and take the time to sample new brands without old biases.

Remember that light lagers in their regions of origin were never the sole style of beer available. Instead, light lagers were brewed for summer months. In winter, many of these brewers switched recipes and brewed darker, heartier lagers, or "winter warmers." Craft brewers understand this chapter of beer history and have re-introduced seasonal specialties (though some styles are now available year-round).

Craft beers may be expensive when compared to mass-market American lagers, but for good reason. Craft beers are brewed with specially roasted barley malts, flavored and bittered with fresh hop flowers, and aged long enough to induce natural carbonation. As a result, the full range of flavors of craft beers, from fruity to sour, toasty to espresso-like bitterness, surprises and delights even the thriftiest drinkers.

Today, American consumers may choose from more than 65 different beer styles and literally hundreds of brands of craft beers. For each style, there are dozens of brands of beer, with tremendous variety in flavor, texture, and alcohol strength that make them versatile accompaniments to food.

As an ingredient, beer enhances flavors in many ways, according to its style. A very bitter ale works in much the same way that lemon juice or vinegar does; a little goes a long way toward perking up the recipe. A light gold lager adds piquancy and tenderness to a fritter batter. Dark robust lagers and ales imbue stews and casseroles with the aroma of barley, while enriching the roasted flavors of the meats and principal ingredients.

Consider this book a map and use it to explore the combined flavors of beer and food, through cooking with beer.

## TASTE AND THE BEER STYLE

Traditionally, beer is made from four basic ingredients: malted barley, water, hops, and yeast. Wheat or rye may also be used in traditional Bavarian or Belgian beers. The specific kinds of ingredients and brewing techniques yield an immense array of flavors and styles.

What is a "beer style"? The style of a beer refers to the way it was brewed and aged, the expected range of alcohol strength, its bitterness from hops, and the resulting flavors in the finished beer that make the style unique. Knowing the style of a beer lets the drinker make an educated guess at its taste in the glass—and the flavors it will contribute as an ingredient. Look at the basic four ingredients for clues to the style of a beer.

First and foremost, the ingredient that defines the brewing cycle is the yeast. Ale yeasts quickly convert sugar to alcohol at room temperature (60–70°F), so that an ale can be ready to drink in as little as seven to ten days. Ales may taste somewhat fruity, thanks to the powerful yeast. In contrast, lager yeasts are slower to ferment and its yeast requires cooler temperatures (45–50°F). Thus, a traditional lager needs aging at cold temperatures for weeks to months to properly develop clean, crisp flavors. Wild yeasts from the atmosphere are used to ferment Belgian lambic ales and gueuze, with the results being highly sour, complex flavors.

Second, another set of flavors develops from the choice of "malts," or grains used to brew the beer. Barley and wheat are the common grains that provide sugars necessary to make beer, although corn, rice, and rye also are used.

Malts are produced by dampening the grain kernels, allowing them to sprout or to germinate, roasting them slowly, and then grading them by color and fermentable sugar content. For example, "chocolate malt" refers not to a milkshake, but rather to a very dark-roasted barley malt that looks and tastes bitter and toasty, similar to the taste of unsweetened cocoa.

During the brewing cycle, malt kernels are cracked and steeped in hot water to yield a sort of grain "tea." This liquid is full of the sugars necessary to feed the yeast to create both alcohol and carbonation. Any sugars that are not fermented remain in the finished beer, making it taste slightly sweet and often producing a thick or syrupy texture on the tongue.

The third important flavor contribution comes from a twining vine that is a botanical cousin to hemp: hops. Most people either love them or hate them, since hops in beer contribute the bitter, mouth-puckering flavors. Hops are the flowers of the hops vine and contain resins that may smell mild and perfumed, or aromatic as do pine or cedar boughs, or zesty as does the rind of a grapefruit. In general, American hops are famous for their citrusy character, British hops tend to be more earthy and robust, and European hops have more herbal or floral character. People who have tasted bad beer are turned off by the rancid flavors created by stale hops.

Fourth, and most important, the flavors of a beer may change after bottling depending on how carefully it has been treated. Beer is a fragile, perishable product. When exposed to light, oxygen, or high heat, it can develop off-flavors. Yet, beer that is served ice cold often lacks the full aromas and flavors possible if served 10–15°F warmer. See Appendix B (pages 137–139) for guidelines on the best treatment of beer.

The styles of beer most often listed as ingredients in this book include:

BROWN ALE. Perhaps the most ancient style of beer brewed on earth, brown ales are malty and often mild (even a little thin) on the palate; they may be sweet or slightly tangy. Brown ale is a versatile ingredient.

FRUIT ALE. A light ale that is either fermented or flavored with the addition of real fruit purées or extracts; in the United States, usually with a tart, somewhat dry finish thanks to the use of wheat malt. In Europe and the United States, some fruit ales are made with sweetened fruit syrup. Fruit ales work well in marinades.

PALE ALE. A golden to copper-colored ale, so named because it is lighter in color, somewhat fruity in flavor, and usually better carbonated than darker porter, Scotch, and stout ales. In cooking, try to use a very lightly hopped American pale ale, since the India pale ale and ESB (extra special bitter) styles are indeed very bitter.

AMBER OR RED ALE. A reddish to auburn-colored ale that often tastes much sweeter than a pale ale, since it is usually made with additional caramel malt or extract to achieve the dark red hue.

TRIPLE BOCK AND BARLEYWINE. Thick, syrupy, and almost sherry tasting, triple bock is an American style of ale produced by Samuel Adams as a seasonal offering. Do not confuse this with the European Abbey or Trappist ale style known as a trippel, which refers to the alcohol strength and aging of the trippel ale. Barleywines are extra-strong ales, often produced for winter holidays.

**PORTER.** Named after the servants who carried casks of this ale into old English taverns, porter is a dark brown ale, rounded and full-bodied, but not usually quite as heavy and bitter as a stout.

**SCOTCH ALE.** A very robust, almost syrupy dark ale that is brewed with lots of malt for a higher alcohol content. Thick and palate-coating, a Scotch ale can be paired with rich foods, such as spicy barbecue or sweet chocolate, and still maintain its flavor. High in alcohol, Scotch ales are usually served in small glasses shaped like thistles, the national symbol of Scotland.

**STOUT.** Usually brewed with even darker roasted chocolate malts or black roasted barley to create a drink that is almost black in the glass. Stouts may be dry and bitter, smooth and sweet, or even somewhat toasty or coffee-like in flavor. Stouts may also be brewed with lactose, or milk sugar. The result is a creamy, sweetish stout known as milk stout.

**BOCK LAGER.** Contrary to myths, bock beers are not the residue at the bottom of the brewing vessels or aging tanks. Brewed with two or three times as much malt as a standard lager beer, bock lagers are full of malt sweetness and toasted grain flavors, although some strong bocks are also very bitter due to generous use of hops. Bock beers tend to be high in alcohol, which results in peppery aromas, so pair these with pungent flavors. Doppelbocks are extra-strong versions of this lager.

**DUNKEL LAGER.** A reddish-brown lager beer that can be somewhat bready and malty, due to typically light hopping rates. Dunkels are excellent to use when cooking onions, garlic, and leeks, since the caramelized flavors of these root vegetables accentuate the soothing sweetness of the malt.

**PILSNER LAGER.** The style of light lager that inspired most of the well-known American brands of lager, Pilsner beers can be very malty, crisp, and bitter (as in the original Czech brews) or light, mild, and overwhelmingly carbonated (as in the adapted mainstream North American brews). Pilsners make good companions to grilled foods, and in the most highly hopped versions, accentuate spicy Asian flavors and chilies.

WEIZEN OR WEISS (PRONOUNCED "VICE"). "Weiss" refers to an unfiltered wheat beer's cloudy, white haze. "Weizen" refers to the wheat malt used to make this beer. Weiss beers can be clove-like and sour, or sparkling and dry, with a lemony aftertaste. A refreshing style of beer originally brewed as a summertime specialty, weiss beer may be added whenever a spicy or citric flavor is desired. Watch out for hefe-weiss beers: the yeast cells in the unfiltered beer can create off-flavors when boiled.

FRUIT LAMBIC. Traditionally made with wild yeasts, and often fermented with real fruit, lambics are mouth-puckering and complex in flavor. Fruit lambics possess the aroma of the fruit used in brewing, typically cherries, berries, or peaches. Some of the imported lambics destined for the American market are sweetened with syrup or sugar before bottling to suit our national sweet tooth. Not all lambics are made with fruit, but only the fruited styles are used as ingredients in this book.

## WHEN BEER IS BEST USED AS AN INGREDIENT

Cooking with beer is common in the regions of Nord-Pas de Calais, Flanders, Alsace, and throughout Belgium, where many of the world's most fascinating styles of beers are brewed. Northern European cooks celebrate the flavors of beer in everything from a sweet dessert sauce, to a glaze for seared chops, to a marinade for vegetables destined for roasting over an open fire, to an aromatic loaf of bread.

Here in the United States, beer adds distinction to many dishes, from a robust onion soup made with dark porter beer, beef stock, and plenty of caramelized onions, to a melting cheddar cheese rarebit, made with pungent ale and lots of pepper, to accompany snack toasts.

The elemental flavors of beer—bitterness from hops, sweetness of malt, and the yeasty bite of the fermented brew with its tenderizing enzymes—all have their uses in cooking.

**BITTER HOPS.** When cooking with a hoppy India pale ale or ESB, use it sparingly (as you would a squeeze of lemon juice or splash of vinegar) in dishes that require the balance of acidity to counteract rich buttery, oily, or cheesy flavors.

**MALT.** When cooking with a very malty beer, such as a bock lager or mild brown ale, try adding caramelized onions, root vegetables high in sugars such as carrots or shallots, or braised mushrooms as complements in your recipe.

**YEAST.** When cooking with a yeasty beer, such as an unfiltered wheat beer, try including it in baked goods or sauces where its yeasty bite will enhance the other flavors, as well as contribute to the texture.

**FRUITY FLAVORS.** When cooking with a fruit ale or lager, add more fresh fruit to enhance the flavors if making a sweet dessert; fruit-flavored ales may also be used to poach fish or make a delicate mopping sauce for barbecued chicken or turkey.

When cooking with beer, these techniques work well:

**BAKE.** Beer breads are a mainstay for most cooks who enjoy beer as an ingredient, since its malty, fermented flavors match the yeasty flavors of raised breads, rolls, and even sweet pastries.

**BATTERS.** All kinds of foods battered with beer and flour, from apple fritters, to spicy deep-fried onion rings, to seafood such as scallops, get light texture and tender crusts from the carbonation and unfiltered yeast cells found in certain styles of beer. Add beer to savory pancake, crêpe, and waffle batters for good crumb and texture.

**BRAISE.** Slow, gentle oven braising in a blend of beer and stock or other cooking liquid yields wonderful stews and fork-tender meats such as corned beef and pot roast.

**DEGLAZE.** Mix a half cup of beer in the bottom of a roasting pan full of drippings to make a light glaze for roasted meats; try this with roast pork and a dark ale such as stout.

**GELÉE OR JELLED SAUCES.** Blend beer with unflavored gelatin and a little water, fruit juice, or stock to create a sweet or savory gelée or jellied accompaniment to fruit desserts, pastries, or poached fish. A raspberry and lambic gelée makes a wonderful garnish for poached salmon.

**MACERATE.** Plump up dried fruits, such as cranberries, currants, raisins, and apples, by soaking them overnight in a complementary fruit-flavored ale or spicy, dry lager or barleywine, and add them to fruit compotes or baked goods. Soak dried mushrooms in ale to add flavor.

**MARINATE.** Add tenderness and flavor to tough cuts of meat by marinating them in beers that pair well with the sauce. Interestingly, fruit flavors such as peach ale go well with barbecue, standing in for the sweet cider vinegar in a marinade or mop sauce.

**POACH.** Fish filets, sausages, and other proteins may be poached in beer for extra flavor, provided the temperature remains between 160°F and 180°F.

**SIMMER.** Beer in soups, chilies, and stews can be reduced at very low heat, provided there are complementary sugars in root vegetables or other sweet ingredients to offset the effect of concentrating the bitter hops.

**SPRITZ.** Gently spray a mild lager, which has been poured into a misting bottle, on wild greens to give them flavor and aroma without overwhelming the palate. A spritz of beer stirred into a sauce at the end of cooking can be the finishing touch that enhances its flavor.

But, remember, all beers are not designed to be added to all dishes. The same live yeast cells that create a fruity effervescence in a Trappist ale can create havoc when cooked into a sauce that must be simmered for a long time, or reduced over high heat. In general, reduce the volume of beer by no more than one-third to prevent off-flavors from developing.

Hops also represent a culinary challenge to a chef or home cook. Highly hopped beers, such as robust ESB ales, are not suited to cooking techniques that call for boiling or for long simmering. Hops may take on the aroma of overcooked cabbage, or become somewhat stale tasting when boiled or overcooked.

When I apprenticed in the kitchens of In't Spinnekopke, Brussels, the master chef, Jean Rodriguez, taught me that beer is best used when its natural acidity complements or replaces the acidity of another ingredient, such as lemon juice. He used potent Trappist ales as ingredients in sauces by balancing hops bitterness with the natural sugars present in root vegetables or fruits, or even by adding a teaspoon or two of sugar. Sometimes the master chef added a bit of cognac or rum to balance the bitterness of beer in a concentrated sauce.

Chef Jonathan Zearfoss of the Culinary Institute of America, Hyde Park, New York, cautions against adding beer for the mere sake of preparing a food with beer: "To make the beer contribute significantly to the final flavor of the dish requires some thought and planning."  The recipes chosen for this book do much of that planning for you.

In general, I avoid cooking everything in a meal with beer. This flies in the face of brewpub promotions, which often feature special brewmaster menus where every single dish is prepared with beer. (In defense, I know of few wine lovers who would insist on preparing every course of a wine-tasting dinner with wine as an ingredient!) Also, it's perfectly fine to use one beer for cooking a dish and choose another to serve with it as a beverage. As Chef Zearfoss puts it: "One of the most prevalent myths is that one must pair a dish prepared with beer with the same beer used in cooking. You wouldn't pair a pasta topped with tomato sauce with tomato juice."

## WHEN BEER IS BEST PAIRED WITH FOOD

Since every palate is different, beware of blanket recommendations. To my taste, mussels are wonderful with a dark lager,

but the classic recommendation is to eat shellfish with stout. Each of the recipes that follows includes a recommended pairing from my palate's perspective—yours may be different, and that's to be expected and respected.

That said, everybody needs a little guidance. The following advice will help you think about flavors in the same way a professional chef does.

"Cut, complement, and contrast" are the "three Cs" of any food and beverage pairing. The acidity of the hops in a beer often cuts through rich flavors, such as buttery, aged cheddar cheese. The sweet, malty flavor of a dark lager can complement the caramel flavors of slowly sautéed onions in an onion soup. A dark, toasty porter will contrast with the mild, somewhat briny flavors of steamed shrimp.

Chef Zearfoss advises thinking about the flavor of a beer and imagining the foods that would go with it. When you taste a beer for the first time, appreciate its flavor on its own, then picture the kinds of food you would like to taste with it. Keep your beer and food combinations in mind as you plan your menus. When you taste the dish, you will discover whether the experiment was successful.

Most families plan meals around whatever's available in the refrigerator, not the beer they plan to drink. With that reality comes a different strategy. If you have fixed your meal, and are now contemplating the choice of a beer to go with it, consider your palate's preferences.

In short, what tastes do you want to emphasize? Apply the principle of the three Cs to your menu. If you have made a terrifically spicy chili, you might want to pair it with a beer that provides a refreshing contrast, such as a mild golden lager or a fruity amber ale. But if you consider yourself a true fan of hot and spicy foods, you could choose a robust, highly hopped, and somewhat peppery ESB ale that will complement and enhance fiery flavors.

Certain styles of beer taste best when paired with foods and sparingly used as ingredients. These styles of beer are highly complex, often aged with yeast in the bottle, and high enough in alcohol and body (and price) to make them comparable to wines. Examples include Belgian strong ales, English bottle-conditioned ales, Trappist beers, and German doppelbocks, unfiltered wheat beers, and certain fruit lambic beers.

Considerable character, powerful flavors, and the presence of yeast sediments make such beers challenging and costly as ingredients, but wonderfully adept as partners to a wide range of dishes. When cooking with unfiltered beers of such depth and immense character, add them at the last minute to a cooked dish, or use them in recipes that do not call for long heating. For example, a sweet sabayon dessert sauce, made with lightly warmed and thickened egg yolks whipped with sugar, is wonderful when prepared with a Trappist ale.

In addition to potential culinary pairings, think about the nature of the occasion when choosing a beer as a partner for food. Casual events, gatherings of friends and family, and even large, formal parties can include beer on the menu. A magnum bottle of spiced Christmas ale from the Anchor Brewing Company can hold its place on the holiday table as easily as a six-pack of Pilsner can perch on a picnic table.

A chart of beer styles and brands, organized by flavors first, should help the beginner find appropriate beers, and a glossary of tasting terms should help define the flavors (see Appendix C). Each recipe in this book (with the exception of Easy Appetizers) includes suggested styles for pairing with the completed dish. For more detailed information on beer styles, refer to books such as *The Beer Enthusiast's Guide* by Gregg Smith (Storey Publishing, 1994); *A Taste for Beer* by Stephen Beaumont (Storey Publishing, 1995); or *Michael Jackson's Beer Companion* (Running Press, 1994).

# CHAPTER 2

# SNACKS AND STARTERS

## EASY APPETIZERS

Make the most of beer's convivial style and offer it at the beginning of a meal. A dry, hoppy beer will whet people's appetites for even the simplest finger foods: cheese, vegetables, chips and dips, or crackers and spreads. In fact, beer as a drink to accompany hors d'oeuvres is far more widely accepted than offering beer as a table beverage.

In part, that is because beer is a refreshingly thirst-quenching drink to sip when compared to many other kinds of aperitifs. It will not overpower the senses through extremely tannic flavors, highly citric mixers, or high alcohol content. Many of the world's most popular beers are known as "session beers," because you can drink more than one and still participate intelligently in a conversation.

Any host's goal is to offer beverages that make good partners to the food prepared. The recipes that follow feature the flavors of beer as an ingredient and are compatible with a wide range of beer brands. Here are a few easy appetizers to get you started.

# BEER CHEESE

1 tablespoon mustard seed
1 tablespoon celery seed
1 cup dark Belgian ale
4 ounces cream cheese
$\frac{1}{4}$ teaspoon salt
$\frac{1}{2}$ teaspoon white pepper
$\frac{1}{2}$ pound grated Gouda cheese

Blend in a food processor until smooth. Serve with toasted bread rounds and sliced radishes.

**YIELD: 2 CUPS**

# BEER AND ONION DIP

1 cup white onion, minced
1 tablespoon olive oil
1 teaspoon cracked black pepper
1 teaspoon salt
1 teaspoon hot curry powder
1 tablespoon Lyle's Golden Syrup or honey
$\frac{1}{2}$ cup doppelbock
8 ounces cream cheese
1 tablespoon Worcestershire sauce
Several dashes Tabasco sauce

Cook the onion, olive oil, pepper, salt, curry powder, syrup or honey, and doppelbock in a 9-inch skillet placed over very low heat until most of the beer has evaporated and the onions are golden brown. Whip together the cream cheese, Worcestershire, and Tabasco, then fold in the cooked and cooled onions. Chill and serve with pumpernickel bread rounds or rye chips.

YIELD: 1 CUP

# BEER AND POTATO CRISPS

2 potatoes, finely grated (about 3 cups)
1 egg
3 tablespoons flour
1 small onion, grated
2 scallions, green part only, minced
2 slices Canadian bacon, cooked and minced
1 cup amber ale
2 tablespoons vegetable oil
Salt and pepper to taste

Blend all ingredients together. Heat a nonstick griddle to 425°F. Drop tablespoons of batter onto the griddle and cook until bubbly and browned, then flip over. Serve with a dab of sour cream or mustard dipping sauce.

YIELD: APPROXIMATELY 2 DOZEN

# STUFFED MUSHROOM CAPS

$\frac{1}{4}$ pound spicy ground Italian sausage

$\frac{1}{2}$ cup minced onion

1 teaspoon thyme

$\frac{1}{4}$ cup bread crumbs

12–15 large mushroom caps, cleaned
and stems removed

12 ounces dark lager

Preheat the oven to 400°F. Brown the sausage, onion, and thyme in a 9-inch heavy skillet set over medium heat. Remove from heat and let cool. Mix in the bread crumbs, and stuff the mushroom caps with the mixture. Place the mushroom caps in a shallow baking dish (9x12 glass or ceramic) and fill the dish with the dark lager. Bake for 20 minutes, or until mushrooms are tender.

YIELD: 12–15 CAPS

BEER PAIRINGS FOR APPETIZERS SHOULD BE LIGHT BUT DRY ENOUGH TO STIMULATE APPETITES: A DRY ASIAN LAGER OR CRISP PALE ALE IS VERSATILE ENOUGH TO PAIR WITH CREAMY DIPS, SMOKED FISH, OR EVEN FRIED FOODS

# BEER BATTER FOR FINGER FOODS

Guests always seem to hang out in the kitchen at a party, so why not prepare food that must be served as soon as it is ready? Fritters make divine finger foods. Everything from oysters to corn to cauliflower to zucchini can be dipped in a simple beer batter and quickly fried to feed your guests. Here is a basic beer batter for vegetable fritters: use sturdy cruciferous vegetables such as broccoli florets, cauliflower, or large thick slices of onion. Or, splurge on oysters, and roll the tender oysters in cornmeal before dipping in the batter to get an extra crispy crust.

1 cup flour
$\frac{1}{4}$ cup cornstarch
1 cup pale ale
2 tablespoons very finely minced red bell pepper
2 tablespoons minced capers
Salt and pepper to taste

Whisk all the ingredients together. Refrigerate until ready to use. See pages 81-82 for instructions on frying. Dip the vegetable pieces or seafood into the batter and fry in small batches. Serve with a splash of hot pepper sauce.

YIELD: 1$\frac{1}{2}$ CUPS BATTER

# PORK SATAY WITH PEANUT ALE SAUCE

*Throughout Asia, the least expensive cuts of meat are often marinated in a satay spice blend, threaded onto skewers, grilled, and sold as street food—sort of Singapore's answer to New York's hot dog carts. Pale ale adds the right zesty bite to complement lemongrass and garlic.*

2 pounds pork bottom round or rump steak
1 cup pale ale
$\frac{1}{2}$ cup real peanut butter (creamy)
1 cup unsweetened coconut milk
1 teaspoon minced coriander leaves
3 slices crystallized ginger (approximately
1 ounce), minced
1 teaspoon dried lemongrass leaves
5 cloves garlic, minced
1 teaspoon red chili pepper flakes (Thai chilies
are most authentic)
Bamboo skewers, soaked in water

1. Trim the pork and cube into $\frac{3}{4}$-inch chunks, then flatten slightly with a clean rubber mallet or the flat side of a cleaver. Place in a gallon-sized zip-seal plastic bag or shallow dish.

2. Mix the pale ale, peanut butter, coconut milk, coriander leaves, ginger, lemongrass leaves, garlic, and chili flakes in a quart-sized bowl (or blend in a food processor for a perfectly smooth sauce). Reserve $\frac{1}{2}$ cup of this sauce in a glass dish and seal with plastic wrap.

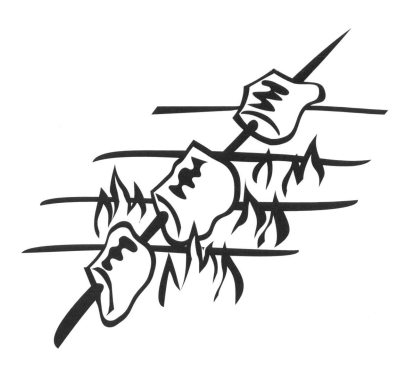

3. Pour the remainder of the sauce over the meat and seal the bag or cover the dish. Shake to distribute marinade evenly, and then chill both the sauce and meat mixture overnight.

4. Thread 4–5 chunks of meat on each skewer, piercing through the flattened edges so the meat will lie flat on the grill surface.

5. Grill for 8–10 minutes over a hot wood charcoal fire; cooking time varies with the thickness of the meat. Serve as an appetizer with the reserved satay sauce, which may be thickened with a few more teaspoons of peanut butter if desired.

YIELD: 5–6 SERVINGS
PAIRING: DRY ASIAN LAGER

# CHEDDAR PEPPER WAFERS

*Make a batch of this dough, and keep it sealed in the refrigerator. Slice and bake only as many wafers as you want to serve that evening, since these little crisps taste best when served warm. You can even bake just two or three wafers for yourself in a toaster oven. Its inspiration comes from the "cheese pennies" popular in the 1950s for cocktail parties; versions of this recipe can be found in just about every community cookbook published in that era.*

½ pound grated aged cheddar (white cheddar
is preferable)

1 teaspoon cayenne pepper

2 tablespoons butter

1 cup flour

1 teaspoon salt

½ teaspoon baking powder

1 cup pecan meal

½ cup India pale ale

1. Blend the cheddar, pepper, butter, flour, salt, baking powder, and $\frac{1}{2}$ cup of the pecan meal in the bowl of a food processor fitted with a metal blade. Pulse on high speed twice, then add the pale ale.

2. Pulse until smooth, about 3–4 more turns. Place a piece of parchment paper 15 inches long on the counter top and sprinkle the remaining pecan meal on the paper. Then use a spatula to scrape dough onto the parchment paper so the pecan meal coats the dough. Gather the sides of the paper together and roll to form logs about $2\frac{1}{2}$ inches in diameter and 10–12 inches long. Roll up the parchment paper and seal. Refrigerate until firm, about 2 hours.

3. Preheat the oven to 400°F. Line a baking sheet with parchment paper. Unwrap the dough.

4. Use a sharp serrated knife to cut off thin slices of the chilled cheddar dough log.

5. Place the cheddar wafers on the baking sheet and bake for 12–15 minutes, or until bubbly and golden. Serve immediately.

YIELD: $2\frac{1}{2}$ DOZEN WAFERS
PAIRING: AMBER ALE

# PORTER-CHILI PASTE GRILLED SHRIMP

*Briny shrimp turn pungent and smoky when basted and grilled with this marinade. The drier and hoppier the beer, the more intense the chili flavors will be.*

12 ounces porter

$\frac{1}{3}$ cup toasted sesame oil

1 tablespoon frozen lime juice concentrate

2 tablespoons Thai fish sauce

5 cloves garlic, peeled and crushed

2 ounces candied ginger, minced

1 teaspoon powdered cardamom

1 teaspoon Chinese red chili paste

1$\frac{1}{2}$ pounds shrimp (about 30 shrimp),
heads removed, shells on

10 bamboo skewers, soaked in water

1. Blend the porter, sesame oil, lime juice concentrate, fish sauce, garlic, ginger, cardamom, and chili paste, and whisk well.

2. Rinse the shrimp and place in a gallon-sized zip-seal plastic bag, pour the marinade in, seal, and refrigerate overnight.

3. Prepare a grill and thread the shrimp on skewers, three pieces to each skewer. Grill about 40–60 seconds on each side over a hot fire, or watch until the shells just turn orange-pink and the flesh starts to turn opaque white, and take them off the grill.

4. Place on a platter and serve immediately.

YIELD: 10 SKEWERS OF 3 SHRIMP,
ENOUGH FOR 6–8 PEOPLE
PAIRING: DRY AMBER ALE OR
GOLDEN TRAPPIST ALE

# SAUSAGE AND LAGER MEATBALLS

*I save the crusty ends and smallest slices from round loaves of sourdough bread and use them to make fresh bread crumbs. The good flavor and texture of fresh crumbs make them excellent binders for ale-enriched meatballs.*

$\frac{1}{2}$ cup sourdough bread crumbs

$\frac{1}{2}$ cup minced onion

12 ounces bulk Italian sausage (may be medium, hot, or mild)

$\frac{1}{2}$ cup amber lager

2 tablespoons minced pimiento or roasted red pepper

2 tablespoons minced parsley

1 teaspoon red pepper flakes (reduce this by half if using spicy sausage)

Semolina flour (pasta flour)

Peanut oil for frying (about 1 cup)

1. Fit a food processor with a metal blade. Blend the bread crumbs, onion, sausage, lager, pimiento or roasted red pepper, parsley, and red pepper flakes, using short pulses of the food processor, until well mixed (but not pasty). Transfer to a mixing bowl, cover with plastic wrap, and chill the mixture for 30 minutes.

2. Use a teaspoon to form 24–30 meatballs. To ease rolling and shaping, place a mounded teaspoon of sausage mixture on a plate dusted with about $\frac{1}{2}$ cup semolina flour. Roll the meat into a ball, using the flour to keep it from sticking to your hands. Place the meatballs on a baking sheet lined with wax paper.

3. Preheat the oven to 325°F. Heat peanut oil in a deep 10-inch heavy skillet to frying temperature (about 350°F). Brown the meatballs in batches of 8–10 meatballs, and turn quickly to keep them from burning or sticking together. The meatballs will be crispy and browned, but not cooked through.

4. Place the browned meatballs on an unlined baking sheet and bake for 15–20 minutes, or until cooked through. Drain the meatballs on paper towels while assembling the serving tray.

5. Place the meatballs on small rounds of pumpernickel bread spread with hot mustard, and serve with baby dill pickles and sliced radishes.

YIELD: 8 SERVINGS AS AN APPETIZER
PAIRING: CRISP, WELL-HOPPED LAGER

# ARTICHOKE AND CHEESE DIP

*Beer may be used to replace the fat in certain dishes—and this is a good example. Artichoke hearts and Parmesan cheese are bound not by mayonnaise and eggs, but by beer, bread crumbs, and egg white for a much less caloric version of this popular baked dip.*

1¾ pounds artichoke hearts (2 14-ounce cans, drained, or equal quantity frozen and thawed)

1 cup freshly grated Parmesan cheese

1 tablespoon minced lemon zest

1 tablespoon cracked black pepper

Several drops hot pepper sauce

8 ounces light cream cheese (neufchatel)

1 egg white

½ cup plain bread crumbs

1 cup amber ale

1. Preheat oven to 350°F. Blend all the ingredients in a food processor fitted with a metal blade. Scrape the mixture into a 2-quart baking dish and bake for 30 minutes, or until browned and bubbly at the edges.

2. Serve with carrot and celery sticks, chips made from torn green cabbage leaves, or slices of bell pepper or toasted rye or pumpernickel bread.

YIELD: 4 CUPS DIP, FOR 12 PEOPLE
PAIRING: BELGIAN GOLDEN ALE OR BELGIAN WIT

# CHICKEN TENDERS WITH COFFEE STOUT GLAZE

*Chicken glazed in a dark, sweet stout sauce makes a terrific starter for an Asian stir-fry or topping for a soba noodle dish. The stout is not actually made with coffee beans; instead, it should taste like espresso. This dish may be served hot or cold.*

1½ pounds chicken thighs, skins removed and trimmed of all visible fat

12 ounces coffee stout

1 teaspoon salt

1 teaspoon white pepper

3 cloves garlic

⅓ cup orange juice concentrate

2 tablespoons Lyle's Golden Syrup or dark corn syrup

Garnish: toasted sesame seeds and minced green scallions

1. Rinse and pat dry the chicken pieces. Preheat the oven to 350°F. Place the chicken in a buttered 9x11-inch baking dish. Blend the remaining ingredients, except the garnish, and pour over the chicken.

2. Bake the chicken at 350°F, stirring and basting often, for 30–45 minutes, depending on the size of the pieces. Turn several times, so that the glaze is evenly baked on the chicken.

3. Remove from oven and let cool for 10–15 minutes before garnishing.

YIELD: 6–8 SERVINGS
PAIRING: AMBER LAGER OR KÖLSCH

"It was as natural
as eating and to me
as necessary, and I would
not have thought of
eating a meal
without drinking... Beer."

Ernest Hemingway

# CHAPTER 3

# SOUPS AND STEWS

soups and stews are natural companion foods for beer, since its malty flavors and light carbonation provide a welcome contrast to the rich meat or cheese flavors in these dishes. Soups and stews may make a light meal for a lunch, with the addition of a salad or sandwich, or stand alone as a course in a more formal dinner.

Be aware that soups and stews made with beer tend to become more bitter with reheating. That is because the hops flavor becomes concentrated as the other liquids evaporate during heating. For that reason, try to package any leftover soup or stew in microwave-safe, single-serving-size containers. That way, you won't be increasing the bitterness of the soup by reheating an entire pot, when all you really want is enough for your lunch.

# WISCONSIN CHEESE SOUP

*Flavored with two kinds of cheese, this soup makes a satisfying lunch, along with open-faced sandwiches of sliced tomatoes and smoked ham.*

8 ounces grated cheddar cheese (medium aged)

2 ounces crumbled gorgonzola or blue cheese

2 tablespoons butter

1 tablespoon flour

2 cups defatted chicken broth

1 teaspoon dried thyme

$\frac{1}{2}$ cup half-and-half

1 cup ESB ale

Salt and pepper to taste

1.  Let the cheeses warm to room temperature on a sheet of wax paper.

2.  Melt the butter in a 2-quart heavy nonstick saucepan placed over medium heat. Sprinkle in the flour and whisk well. The flour and butter should just begin to brown before adding other ingredients.

3.  Whisk in the chicken broth, bit by bit. At first the mixture will seem lumpy, but keep stirring as you add more broth and it will become smooth. Add the thyme. Simmer and stir until slightly thickened and smooth. Remove from heat.

4.  When the soup base is no longer steaming hot (about 5 minutes), slowly whisk in the half-and-half. Add the cheese in $\frac{1}{4}$ cups, whisking well after each addition. Return the saucepan to the stove, placing it over medium-low heat.

5.  Whisk in the ESB ale and the salt and pepper. Continue to whisk the soup until it is completely smooth and the cheeses are melted; it should be steaming, but not simmering or boiling. Do not let the soup boil: this will cause the proteins in the cheese to coagulate and you will wind up with a stringy mess. Serve with garlic croutons or fresh sourdough baguettes on the side.

YIELD: 4 SERVINGS
PAIRING: INDIA PALE ALE OR AMBER ALE

# SCOTCH ALE SOUP

*The malty richness of Scotch ale accentuates the sturdy beef and barley base of this thick soup.*

3 tablespoons olive oil

2 cups finely chopped onions

1 teaspoon dried savory

1 teaspoon celery seed

4 cups defatted chicken broth

$\frac{1}{2}$ ounce dried mushrooms, soaked and grit removed

$\frac{1}{2}$ cup pearl barley

3 tablespoons peanut oil

1 pound round steak

1 cup peeled and sliced carrots (2 medium carrots)

Salt and freshly ground pepper to taste

1 cup Scotch ale or extra stout ale

1. Place the olive oil in a 1-gallon heavy Dutch oven and place over medium heat.

2. Add the onions and sauté until they caramelize to a golden brown; stir often to prevent burning or sticking. Add the savory and celery seed.

3. Stir in the chicken broth, dried mushrooms, and barley. Simmer about 45 minutes.

4. While the soup base simmers, place a heavy 10-inch skillet over high heat and pour in the peanut oil.

5. Bring the oil to the smoking point, then add the round steak and sear on both sides. When both sides are seared with a brown crust, remove from heat. Cut into cubes and reserve the juices and pan drippings.

6. When the mushrooms and barley are tender, add the carrots, salt and pepper to taste, and the cubed steak and reserved juices. Stir and cook for 15 minutes more, or until the carrots are tender. Deglaze the steak sauté pan with the ale, then scrape all into the Dutch oven. Simmer 5 minutes, or until warmed through. Serve with crusty bread.

YIELD: 6 SERVINGS
PAIRING: DARK LAGER

# BLACK BEAN CHILI

*This chili uses plenty of ground beef and garlic, and is more stewlike than soupy. The smoky heat of the chipotle chilies (available canned or dried) is accented by the addition of a smoked malt beer, such as a rauchbier. Add a bit of color by topping with the garnishes suggested below.*

2 small chipotle chilies, canned or dried

2 cups diced mild white onion

4 cloves garlic, minced

2 slices bacon, diced

2 tablespoons olive oil

2 pounds ground beef

2 14 $\frac{1}{2}$-ounce cans black beans (or 4 cups reconstituted and cooked dried black beans)

3 cups beef or vegetable broth

12 ounces smoked beer (rauchbier or blackened malt beer)

1 cup water

2 tablespoons tomato paste

1 tablespoon powdered cumin

Salt to taste

Hot pepper sauce to taste

Garnish: grated cheese, minced scallions, minced fresh cilantro leaves, diced red and green bell peppers, and diced tomatoes

1. Mince the canned chipotle chilies. If using dried chilies, soak them in warm water to cover. When the chilies are soft, remove seeds and mince the chilies. Reserve the soaking liquid to add to the chili base.

2. Sauté the chilies, onion, garlic, and bacon in the olive oil in a 1-gallon stockpot over medium heat. When the onion is soft and translucent, add the ground beef. Brown the ground beef, then skim off any fat left in the pan.

3. Add the black beans, broth, beer, water (including soaking liquid for chilies), tomato paste, and seasonings. Simmer for 1–2 hours, and taste again. If you want more spice, add red pepper flakes in addition to the hot pepper sauce.

4. Ladle the soup into bowls, garnish, and serve.

YIELD: 6–8 SERVINGS
PAIRING: SCOTCH ALE OR DOPPEL BOCK LAGER

# CLASSIC BEEF STEW

*If you make this stew with a dark Trappist ale, you could call it a carbonnade, as the Belgians do. If you make it with the dark ale known as stout, just call it Irish stew.*

4 tablespoons flour

1 teaspoon salt

1 teaspoon white pepper

2 tablespoons olive oil

1½ pounds beef steak for stew, cut into cubes
about 1½ inches, trimmed of fat

2 cups beef broth

12 ounces dark Trappist or dry stout ale

2 bay leaves

3 medium carrots, peeled and sliced

2 medium parsnips, peeled and sliced

1½ cups pearl onions

2 cups peeled and diced potatoes, about 1-inch cubes
(approximately 2 large potatoes)

2 tablespoons minced parsley

1 teaspoon crumbled dried thyme

YIELD: 6 SERVINGS
PAIRING: AMBER ALE OR DARK, MILD LAGER

1. Combine the flour, salt, and white pepper.

2. Place the olive oil in the bottom of a pressure cooker or 1-gallon stockpot, set over medium heat. Heat the oil until it is just beginning to sizzle.

3. Sprinkle the beef with the seasoned flour, shake off the excess, and sauté, stirring often, in the hot oil. Let the meat brown, then reduce the heat and add the broth, ale, bay leaves, carrots, parsnips, onions, potatoes, parsley, and thyme.

4. Cover the pressure cooker and cook at medium pressure for 30 minutes, or cover the stockpot and simmer, stirring often, for 2 hours. Remove from heat, remove the bay leaves, and taste. Adjust seasonings and serve with fresh bread or biscuits.

# SEAFOOD STEW

*In Belgium, chefs make a carbonnade blanche, or seafood stew, with wheat beer, leeks, and shallots. Here is an adaptation of a recipe prepared by chef Jean Rodriguez at In't Spinnekopke, in Brussels.*

1 pound monkfish, boned and cut into cubes

1 pound sea scallops

1 pound mussels, shelled

2 tablespoons butter

2 cups thinly sliced leeks

$\frac{1}{2}$ cup minced shallots

1 cup shredded carrot

1 cup thinly sliced celery

1 tablespoon cognac

$1\frac{1}{2}$ cups heavy cream

2 cups Belgian wit beer (Blanche de Bruges works well)

Salt and white pepper

Garnish: 3 tablespoons minced fresh parsley,
3 tablespoons minced lemon zest

1. Clean the seafood and set aside. Mussels should be rinsed and beards removed with needle-nosed pliers (to protect fingertips from sharp shells). Monkfish should be skinned and bones removed. Your seafood grocer should be able to do this for you.

2. Heat the butter in a 2-quart heavy saucepan. Sauté the leeks, shallots, carrot, and celery for 5 minutes over medium heat. Stir in the cognac and cream, and reduce the heat.

3. Simmer until the vegetables are just tender, about 6 more minutes.

4. Stir in the wit beer and monkfish. Cook over medium heat, stirring often, for 8–10 minutes, then add the scallops and mussels. Cook for an additional 5–7 minutes, or until the shellfish are just cooked but still tender. Taste and adjust seasonings with salt and white pepper.

5. Garnish with the parsley and lemon zest, and serve over buttered rice.

YIELD: 6 SERVINGS
PAIRING: BELGIAN STRONG ALE,
SUCH AS CHIMAY WHITE OR DUVEL

# MILD AND WILD MUSHROOM SOUP

*"Mild" is a style of brown ale very popular in England as a "session" beer, one that is not too high in alcohol and body so that it's possible to drink more than one and still participate in a session of conversation at the pub. It makes a great base for a rich, creamy mushroom soup.*

2 ounces dried white mushrooms, sliced

1 ounce dried wild mushrooms, sliced or chopped

24 ounces mild brown ale (or black and tan, equal parts porter and amber ale)

2 tablespoons butter

2 cloves garlic, minced

3 tablespoons minced shallots

$\frac{1}{4}$ cup powdered milk

1 cup cream

4 cups defatted chicken broth

6 ounces fresh portabello mushrooms, thinly sliced

$\frac{1}{2}$ cup finely grated potato

1 teaspoon dill weed

Salt and pepper to taste

Optional: 1 tablespoon sweet sherry

1. Soak the dried mushrooms in 12 ounces of the ale in a shallow glass dish. Let mushrooms soften, stirring several times. (Best left to soak overnight or for several hours to soften completely.)

2. Place the butter in a deep 2-quart heavy saucepan, and melt over low heat. Stir in the garlic and shallots, and sauté gently, until garlic just begins to turn gold.

3. Whisk together the powdered milk and the cream, until all the milk powder dissolves. Whisk this into the garlic-shallot butter and cook for 2–3 minutes, or until simmering.

4. Stir in the chicken broth and the soaked mushrooms, lifting them out of the brown ale with a slotted spoon to prevent grit from the mushroom gills being added to the soup. Add the remaining 12 ounces of ale to the soup base, with the fresh portabello mushrooms and the grated potato.

5. Season with the dill weed and salt and pepper. Simmer until thickened and the mushrooms are completely tender, about 20–30 minutes. Do not let the soup boil. If the taste seems too bitter, add a tablespoon of sherry to round out the flavors.

YIELD: 6 SERVINGS
PAIRING: DARK LAGER OR AMBER ALE

# PUMPKIN AND AUBURN ALE BISQUE

*When Wisconsin's Leinenkugel introduced its first ale, which is auburn in color and mild in flavor, I was inspired to try a new soup with it—a mellow, slightly spicy pumpkin bisque. Though a traditional bisque soup is loaded with fattening cream and egg yolks to thicken the soup, I used potato starch, blended with half-and-half, to achieve a similar result with less fat and cholesterol. Potato starch is found in supermarkets in the kosher foods or the baking section.*

$\frac{1}{3}$ cup finely minced onion

2 tablespoons butter

1 tablespoon barley malt syrup (Eden Foods packages a food-grade barley malt syrup, or you may substitute honey instead)

1 teaspoon ground cinnamon

Zest of one lemon, yellow skin only, minced

1 15-ounce can pumpkin purée (not seasoned or spiced)

1 14$\frac{1}{2}$-ounce can chicken broth

$\frac{1}{3}$ cup half-and-half

1 teaspoon potato starch

1–1$\frac{1}{4}$ cups amber ale

Salt and white pepper to taste

Garnish: freshly grated nutmeg

YIELD: 6 SERVINGS
PAIRING: FRUITY AMBER ALE

1.  Sauté the onion in the butter in a 2-quart saucepan placed over medium-low heat. The onion should be translucent and just golden. Stir in the barley malt syrup or honey, cinnamon, and lemon zest.

2.  Let the onion simmer 1 minute with the seasonings, then add the pumpkin purée and chicken broth. Reduce the heat to low and simmer, stirring often, for 10–15 minutes to let the flavors meld.

3.  Whisk the half-and-half and potato starch together until smooth, then whisk into the soup base. Simmer, stirring often, until smooth and thickened.

4.  Stir in the ale and blend well. Taste and adjust seasonings. Let the soup warm through completely, then serve with a dusting of freshly grated nutmeg.

# BIG BOCK CHILI

*The rich malty flavors of bock beer contrast with the spicy peppers and chilies used to make this thick soup.*

2 pounds ground beef, preferably
coarse ¼-inch ground chuck
5 cloves garlic, peeled and minced
2 cups peeled and diced white onion
3 jalapeño peppers, seeded and minced
3–5 tablespoons chili powder, to taste
1 teaspoon white pepper
½ teaspoon cayenne pepper
½ teaspoon ground cinnamon
1 teaspoon freshly ground black pepper
1 cup seeded and chopped red bell pepper
1 cup seeded and chopped green bell pepper
1 28-ounce can crushed tomatoes
4 cups cooked and drained beans (try a blend of red
kidney, pinto, and anasazi beans)
1 cup black coffee
12 ounces bock beer
Garnish: fresh minced cilantro or sliced green scallions

1. Brown the beef in a 2-gallon soup pot over medium heat until juices and fat begin to simmer. Add the garlic, onion, jalapeños, and seasonings and continue to simmer until the beef is no longer pink.

2. Add bell peppers, crushed tomatoes, beans, coffee, and beer. Stir well, reduce heat to low, and simmer, uncovered, for one hour until chili is thick. Adjust seasonings if desired. Serve with rice and garnish.

**YIELD: APPROXIMATELY 8 LARGE SERVINGS**
**PAIRING: DARK LAGER OR DOPPELBOCK**

# SHREDDED PORK AND CORN STEW

*The mellow flavors of the hominy corn bring out the sweetness of the tomatoes and malty lager.*

1 cup dried hominy corn or 1 15-ounce can hominy
2 cups diced onion
3 tablespoons minced garlic
2 tablespoons olive oil
4 roasted red peppers, chopped
2 jalapeño peppers, diced
1 28-ounce can chopped tomatoes
1 teaspoon dried oregano
2 tablespoons chili powder
12 ounces light North American
(not reduced-calorie) lager
2 cups cooked pork roast, shredded
Salt and pepper to taste

1. Simmer the dried hominy in 2 cups water for 45 minutes or until most of the water is absorbed and the corn is tender. Remove from heat and let cool. If using canned hominy, drain and rinse, then drain again.

2. Sauté the onion and garlic in the olive oil in a large Dutch oven until the onion is translucent. Add the roasted red peppers, jalapeños, tomatoes, oregano, chili powder, and reserved hominy corn.

3. Stir in the lager and pork. Cook, uncovered, over medium heat until the meat and corn are tender. Season to taste with the salt and pepper. Serve with corn bread or flour tortillas.

YIELD: 6 SERVINGS
PAIRING: DARK LAGER OR BOCK

"I think this would be a good
time for a beer."

Franklin D. Roosevelt

# CHAPTER 4
# SALADS AND SAUCES

## ABOUT BEER DRESSINGS AND SAUCES

The natural acidity of hops creates a bitter bite in beer that can substitute for the acidity of vinegar in a vinaigrette. Some styles of beer are so malty and palate-coating (such as porters, stouts, or Trappist trippel ales) that the amount of oil needed to prepare a tasty dressing can also be reduced. However, some styles of beer are so bold in flavor that just a tiny amount is sufficient in a salad dressing. A Berliner weisse beer or lambic gueuze tastes so acetic, that many Americans think these brews already taste like vinegar. Such mouth-puckering power requires a light touch when blending a dressing, since you want to be able to taste the other ingredients in the salad.

Similarly, all sorts of condiments can be made with beer, including savory or sweet sauces. Of course, mustard is king of all the condiments that take kindly to the flavors of beer. The bite of mustard and the mellowness of malt blend into a spread that most Americans love. Honey weiss beer mustard, stout mustard flecked with brown mustard seeds, searing chili beer mustard . . . the multiple styles of mustards made with beer seem endless.

Salsas made with beer are also popular in today's brew-pubs. Thanks to the almost year-round supply of affordable produce and tropical fruits grown in California, fresh salsas of mango and papaya, laced with jalapeños and drenched in ale, show up as garnishes to grilled fish, tostadas, and other Mexican foods.

Chili sauces or catsups enriched with roasted garlic, ground spices, and dark malty ales work well as sides to dress roasted game or pub burgers. When making the Brazilian green chili and parsley sauce known as churrasco sauce, you can replace a portion of the lemon juice traditionally used with an acidic weiss or chili beer.

There are only a handful of sweet sauces that I make with beer. A hot, buttery caramel sauce made with a bit of stout works well for a turtle sundae, vanilla ice cream spiked with toasted pecans and dusted with malted milk powder and grated chocolate. A frothy concoction of beer, sugar, and egg yolks, whipped until aerated and then lightly cooked, makes a wonderful custard base for a trifle of ladyfinger sponge cakes and very ripe berries.

# HONEY-GINGER ALE DRESSING

$\frac{1}{2}$ cup honey

1 teaspoon cornstarch

1 cup honey ale, at room temperature

2 tablespoons grated fresh ginger

1 clove garlic

$\frac{1}{4}$ cup vegetable oil

$\frac{1}{2}$ teaspoon salt

1 tablespoon poppy seeds

1. Dissolve the honey and cornstarch in the honey ale, then slowly cook in a 1-quart saucepan placed over low heat.

2. Put the ginger, garlic, and vegetable oil in a blender and purée on high until smooth. Whisk this mixture into the honey ale in the saucepan, and cook until slightly thickened.

3. Cool to room temperature, whisk in the salt and poppy seeds, and chill before use.

YIELD: 1$\frac{1}{2}$ CUPS

# CREAMY APPLE ALE DRESSING

$\frac{1}{2}$ cup apple ale or hard cider

2 tablespoons frozen apple juice concentrate

1 teaspoon cornstarch

$\frac{1}{2}$ teaspoon mustard powder

1 cup half-and-half

1 teaspoon celery seed

1 teaspoon cracked black pepper

1. Combine all the ingredients. Whisk until smooth, then cook, stirring constantly, in a 1-quart saucepan until creamy and thickened.

2. While still warm, pour over freshly grated cabbage and sliced apples for an easy coleslaw.

**YIELD: 1$\frac{1}{2}$ CUPS**

# WEISS DIJON DRESSING

*This recipe was adapted from one developed by Keith Dinehart of Chicago Brewing Company.*

$\frac{1}{2}$ cup weiss beer

2 tablespoons Dijon mustard

$\frac{1}{3}$ cup olive oil

1 teaspoon crumbled rosemary

1 teaspoon brown mustard seed (small seeds compared to those of yellow mustard)

1 clove garlic, crushed very fine

½ teaspoon salt

½ teaspoon black pepper

2 teaspoons fresh lemon juice

1. Blend all the ingredients. Chill until ready to serve. Excellent with a plain romaine lettuce salad.

YIELD: 1 SCANT CUP

# CHILI BEER CHURRASCO

12 ounces filtered weizen beer (or if you like hot sauces, use a chili beer, strained)

1 dried red chili, seeds removed (or more chilies, to taste)

2 cups finely chopped white onion

2 large bunches parsley, finely chopped

2 tablespoons minced garlic

Salt and pepper to taste

½ cup fresh lemon juice (2 lemons)

1. Blend all ingredients in a food processor until a thick sauce forms. Coat a 2-pound flank steak and about 2 pounds spicy beef sausages with the sauce. Cover with plastic wrap and marinate overnight. Classically used on beef, but may also be used on pork.

2. Grill the meat and sausages, and simmer any remaining sauce separately. Serve with the heated, thickened sauce.

YIELD: 3 CUPS

# DARK LAGER MUSTARD

*Use whole brown mustard seeds (sold in gourmet food stores or Indian groceries) to make this mustard sauce—great for dunking pretzels as a snack.*

$\frac{1}{4}$ cup brown sugar

1 cup dark lager

2 tablespoons brown mustard seeds

2 tablespoons yellow mustard powder

$\frac{1}{2}$ cup cider vinegar

2 shallots, minced

1 teaspoon salt

$\frac{1}{4}$ teaspoon white pepper

2 egg yolks

2 tablespoons melted butter

1. Blend all the ingredients in a blender, then place in the top of a double boiler over simmering (not boiling) water. Cook until thickened and steaming, about 10 minutes, whisking often to prevent curdling.

2. Let cool to room temperature before chilling. Serve as a condiment for all kinds of meats and deli sandwiches. Keeps up to two weeks in a tightly sealed container in the refrigerator.

**YIELD: 1$\frac{1}{2}$ CUPS**

# PAPAYA AND AMBER ALE SALSA

2 ripe papayas, peeled, seeded, and chopped
2 tablespoons minced sweet onion
2 red jalapeño peppers, seeded and minced
3 tablespoons minced cilantro
$\frac{1}{2}$ cup peeled and minced jicama
$\frac{1}{2}$ cup amber ale
$\frac{1}{4}$ cup vegetable oil
Juice of one lime

1. Stir together all the ingredients and refrigerate overnight. Serve with grilled fish or chicken.

**YIELD: 2 CUPS**

# CARAMEL STOUT SAUCE

4 tablespoons butter
1 cup brown sugar
$\frac{1}{2}$ cup stout, at room temperature
$\frac{1}{4}$ cup cream, at room temperature
1 teaspoon cognac or vanilla extract

1. Melt the butter and brown sugar together in a 2-quart heavy saucepan, stirring constantly with a long-handled wooden spoon. Cook to the soft ball stage (238°F on a candy thermometer), when the mixture will begin to caramelize into a syrup.

2. Stir in the stout, cream, and cognac or vanilla extract. The liquids will spatter a bit as they boil and reduce, so be careful when adding them. Stir well and heat until thickened. Serve over ice cream.

**YIELD: 1 CUP**

# SESAME SPINACH SALAD

*The slightly mineral taste of spinach melds well with the sweet malt flavors of an amber ale. The crumbled halvah (a Middle Eastern sesame candy), sesame oil in the salad dressing, and toasted pecans tossed in amongst the greens give it a slightly nutty taste.*

1 cup pecans

$1\frac{1}{2}$ ounces halvah

4 ounces amber ale

$\frac{1}{4}$ cup sesame oil

2 drops Tabasco sauce

1 teaspoon kosher salt

1 teaspoon fresh lemon juice

Coarsely ground black pepper to taste

2 firm, tart apples, such as Granny Smith or McIntosh

4 cups spinach leaves, washed, stemmed, and torn

1 large red bell pepper, seeded and chopped

2 medium carrots, peeled and grated

3 scallions, minced

1. Toast the pecans and chop them coarsely.

2. Blend the halvah, ale, sesame oil, Tabasco, kosher salt, lemon juice, and black pepper until smooth.

3. Peel, core, and slice the apples. Immediately toss the apples in the dressing (to prevent them from browning) and then toss the spinach and remaining ingredients together.

YIELD: 6 SERVINGS
PAIRING: FRUITY PALE ALE

# GRILLED VEGETABLE SALAD

*A grilled vegetable salad is a delicious, easy way to get your five portions of vegetables in a single dish. Even large, fibrous, end-of-season zucchini have tender, appetizing flavors when grilled with a beer baste.*

## GRILLED SALAD

1 crookneck yellow squash, about 1 pound

1 large zucchini squash, about 1 pound

3 medium onions

6 portabello mushrooms

1 Japanese eggplant (long and narrow)

1 red bell pepper, cored and sliced into wide strips

1 green bell pepper, cored and sliced into wide strips

1 yellow bell pepper, cored and sliced into wide strips

## BEER BASTING SAUCE

1 cup honey ale

2 cloves garlic, minced

2 tablespoons grated fresh ginger

1 tablespoon honey

$\frac{1}{2}$ cup olive oil

$\frac{1}{2}$ teaspoon chili garlic paste (sold in the Asian food section of most supermarkets)

1. Prepare a charcoal fire in a grill. Wash all the vegetables and slice into even thicknesses of approximately $\frac{1}{2}$ inch. (I find slicing the squashes and eggplant lengthwise, into long strips, makes them easier to turn on the grill.) Blend all ingredients for basting sauce.

2. When the coals are ashy and glowing, place vegetables on the grill. Baste the vegetables with the beer sauce as they cook to prevent them from drying out.

3. Place on a platter and serve with grilled fish, chicken, or burgers.

YIELD: 6 SERVINGS AS A SIDE DISH
PAIRING: FRUIT ALE, SUCH AS AN
APRICOT ALE OR PEACH ALE

# STEAK SALAD WITH DUNKEL RYE CROUTONS

*Two favorite techniques for cooking are shared by Alan Skversky, regional executive chef of the HOPS!Bistro and Brewery chain. First, an emulsion of beer and toasted browned butter makes a wonderful beery crouton. Second, a small spray bottle filled with beer is great for gently misting your salad greens. You'll get a light taste of beer without drenching delicate lettuces.*

## STEAK SALAD

1½ to 2 pounds flank steak, pan-seared or grilled to desired degree of doneness

½ cup dunkel beer

¾ cup olive oil

2 tablespoons Dijon mustard

2 teaspoons honey

Salt and pepper to taste

1 cup sliced cucumber

½ cup sliced carrots

1 cup sliced mushrooms

1 cup sliced celery

½ cup sliced scallions

4 cups mixed greens

Freshly ground black pepper

## DUNKEL RYE CROUTONS

4 tablespoons butter

4 tablespoons dunkel or dark lager

2 tablespoons finely grated Parmesan or asiago cheese

2 large slices hearty dark rye bread or pumpernickel

1. Slice the cooked steak on the diagonal and place in a large shallow serving dish.

2. Blend the beer, olive oil, mustard, and honey. Season the mixture with salt and pepper to taste and pour over the steak.

3. Stir in the sliced vegetables (except greens), cover and refrigerate.

4. To make the croutons, brown the butter in a heavy skillet and remove from heat to cool. When cooled but still liquid, whisk in the dunkel beer and cheese. Dredge the slices of bread (both sides) in the beer-butter emulsion and grill on a nonstick griddle or cast-iron skillet.

5. When crisp on both sides, remove bread from skillet and cut into cubes.

6. Place the greens on serving plates (1 cup on each plate). Mound the marinated vegetables and sliced steak on top, dividing evenly among the plates. Top with the dunkel rye croutons, and grind fresh pepper over the salads before serving.

YIELD: 4 ENTREE SALADS
PAIRING: DUNKEL WEIZEN BEER

# SMOKED TURKEY AND WILD RICE SALAD

*The smoky flavors of porter and smoked turkey breast are rounded out by the nutty notes of wild rice and fresh, tart grapes. This easy salad can serve as a side dish or entrée, and keeps for days in the refrigerator.*

1 piece smoked turkey, sliced $\frac{1}{2}$-inch thick
(about 12 ounces)
$\frac{1}{2}$ cup porter
2 cups hot cooked wild rice
1 cup seedless red grapes, sliced in half
1 cup sliced celery
$\frac{1}{2}$ cup thinly sliced radishes
1 cup julienne strips of peeled jicama
2 medium carrots, peeled and cut into julienne strips
$\frac{1}{2}$ cup minced parsley
$\frac{1}{2}$ cup minced watercress
$\frac{1}{4}$ cup olive oil
3 tablespoons fresh lemon juice
Kosher salt and cracked black pepper to taste

YIELD: 4–6 SERVINGS
PAIRING: CRISP, DRY LAGER

1. Place a heavy 10-inch skillet over very high heat and sear the turkey on each side. Pour in the porter, let warm for 1 minute, then remove from heat. Set skillet aside to cool.

2. Stir the porter not absorbed by the smoked turkey into the wild rice. Chop the turkey into bite-sized pieces and add to the rice.

3. Toss the wild rice and smoked turkey with the remaining ingredients, and season to taste. Serve on a bed of wild greens.

# POTATO SALAD WITH ALT-CARAWAY DRESSING

*Alt beer is the result of combined ale and lager brewing techniques. It is a lagered or cold-aged beer with the fruity flavors of an ale. The flavor is well suited to marinades and dressings.*

## DRESSING

$\frac{1}{4}$ cup olive oil

$\frac{1}{3}$ cup alt beer

3 ounces light cream cheese (neufchatel)

1 teaspoon caraway seeds

$\frac{1}{2}$ teaspoon celery seed

1 teaspoon kosher salt

$\frac{1}{4}$ teaspoon red pepper flakes

2 tablespoons minced fresh parsley

1. Blend all the ingredients in a blender and set in refrigerator to chill.

## SALAD

1¾–2 pounds small, red new potatoes
1 cup chopped celery (2 stalks)
½ cup peeled, seeded, and diced cucumber
3 scallions, minced (including green parts)
⅓ cup chopped kosher dill pickle
6–8 radishes, sliced
Salt and pepper to taste

1. Boil the potatoes in 1 quart water until tender.

2. Place the vegetables (except potatoes) and dressing in a large bowl and mix well. Remove potatoes from the heat and drain well in a 2-quart colander. When cool enough to handle, cut potatoes into quarters.

3. Toss the warm potatoes with the vegetables and dressing and let cool. Season to taste with salt and pepper. Makes a great side dish for barbecued meats or poultry.

YIELD: 6 SERVINGS
PAIRING: DARK LAGER OR DOPPELBOCK

"Wine is but single broth,
ale is meat, drink, and cloth."

16th Century English Proverb

# CHAPTER 5
# MEAT AND CHICKEN

Meat and poultry harmonize with the flavors of beer added to marinades, spice rubs, basting sauces, and savory or spicy garnishes. When prepared with beer as an ingredient, a marinade serves as a tenderizer as well as a flavor enhancer. Mellow malt flavors and slightly acidic hops help jazz up the plain meat and poultry.

Yet the unifying flavors in the dishes that follow often come from other ingredients as well. You'll notice lots of ethnic chilies, spices such as turmeric or ginger, fruits such as apricot and orange, and herbs such as thyme or cilantro, which serve as top notes in the composition of these dishes.

# AMBER-ORANGE CHICKEN

*Although the glaze in this recipe produces a luscious, amber-colored bird, it requires a dark lager to make it.*

1 6–8 pound roasting chicken

12 ounces dark lager

2 tablespoons sweet paprika

3 tablespoons molasses

1 tablespoon ground turmeric

1 teaspoon white pepper

4 cloves roasted garlic (see page 74)

$\frac{1}{4}$ cup Cointreau or other orange liqueur

1 tablespoon freshly squeezed orange juice

Garnish: 3 tablespoons minced parsley chopped
with 1 tablespoon minced orange zest

1. Preheat the oven to 400°F. Wash and clean the chicken. Blend together the lager, paprika, molasses, turmeric, white pepper, garlic, liqueur, and orange juice in a blender on high speed.

YIELD: 6 SERVINGS
PAIRING: BROWN ALE

2. Place the chicken in a 13x9-inch roasting pan and pour the basting sauce over it. Place in the oven and immediately reduce the heat to 325°F. Roast for about 20 minutes, then begin basting the bird with the pan juices. Roast for 40 more minutes, basting 3–4 more times to ensure the bird roasts to a nice amber color.

3. Garnish and serve with buttered rice.

# APRICOT ALE AND PAPRIKA CHICKEN

*Best made with Pyramid Apricot Ale, this recipe is adapted for cooks outside the brewery's distribution area.*

½ cup apricot nectar

¾ cup amber ale

3 tablespoons apricot fruit spread

2 teaspoons mild paprika

1 teaspoon hot curry powder

4 boneless chicken breasts, slightly flattened
to even thickness

Salt and pepper to taste

1. Preheat the oven to 325°F. Blend the apricot nectar, ale, fruit spread, paprika, and curry in a 1-quart mixing bowl. Whisk well to blend.

2. Place the chicken breasts in a ceramic casserole dish, and cover with the apricot ale blend.

3. Bake for 35–45 minutes, or until the chicken is done. Turn the breasts twice while cooking to ensure they do not dry out. Season with salt and pepper to taste. Serve with Twice-Baked Potatoes (see page 104).

YIELD: 4 SERVINGS
PAIRING: PALE ALE

# GINGERED WEISS CHICKEN

*The August Schell Brewery in New Ulm, Minnesota, brews several different weiss beers; for this recipe, I used their Weizen beer, but you could use almost any filtered wheat beer. Steer clear of the immensely sour Berliner weisse beers, however; the ginger will not compensate for the acetic notes in that style.*

*You may also make this recipe without candied ginger by replacing half the beer in the recipe with an authentic non-alcoholic ginger beer, such as Reed's Jamaican Ginger Beer.*

1 4–5-pound chicken, cut in pieces
1 tablespoon olive oil
16 ounces wheat beer
4 tablespoons candied ginger (about 2 ounces)
Salt and pepper to taste

1. Preheat the oven to 300°F. Wash and pat the chicken dry. Rub with the olive oil and place in a large, deep-rimmed roasting pan.

2. Place 4 ounces of the wheat beer in a blender, add the candied ginger, and cover. Hold cover with a towel and blend on high speed for 1–2 minutes, or until the ginger is dissolved.

3. Stir the gingered beer into the remaining 12 ounces of wheat beer and pour over the chicken.

4. Bake for 1 hour, or until tender. Baste several times during roasting. Add salt and pepper to taste.

YIELD: 4–6 SERVINGS
PAIRING: PALE ALE OR BLACK AND TAN

# ITALIAN SAUSAGE AND POLENTA

*Polenta taragna, a blend of buckwheat and corn flours, usually cooked with butter and cheese, is an Italian peasant dish that adapts surprisingly well to cooking with beer. Several companies sell the preblended polenta taragna as a boxed mix, but if you cannot find it, use one cup yellow cornmeal blended with ⅓ cup buckwheat, ground into a coarse flour.*

2 cups water

8 ounces polenta taragna

16 ounces amber ale

4 spicy Italian sausages

4 tablespoons butter

$\frac{1}{3}$ cup good quality aged Parmesan, cut into slivers

1. Bring the water to a boil in a deep 2-quart saucepan. Stir in the polenta taragna and 8 ounces of the ale. Simmer and stir until the polenta is cooked and creamy, about 20 minutes. Add more beer if the mixture seems too thick.

2. Place the Italian sausages and the remaining 8 ounces of amber ale in a 10-inch skillet. Cook over medium heat. Poach sausages gently until the beer evaporates, then brown on all sides, about 15–20 minutes total cooking time.

3. Stir the butter and cheese into the hot, creamy polenta and keep stirring until the cheese is completely melted. Serve the polenta warm, with the Italian sausage and a tossed salad.

YIELD: 4 SERVINGS
PAIRING: ITALIAN RED LAGER

# PORTER-HOISIN PORK ROAST

*Hoisin, also known as Peking sauce or spicy brown bean sauce, is made from garlic, chilies, and fermented soybeans. It is thick and pungent, and makes a lovely brown crust when basted over roasted pork.*

4 pounds boneless pork roast
12 ounces porter
$\frac{1}{3}$ cup hoisin

1. Preheat oven to 350°F. Line the bottom and sides of a roasting pan with heavy aluminum foil. Place pork roast on the foil. Mix the porter and hoisin. Baste the pork roast with about $\frac{1}{4}$ of this mixture and place in the oven.

2. Roast the pork for 1 hour and 15 minutes, basting at 15–20-minute intervals with the porter-hoisin sauce. When pork roast is done (internal temperature 160°F), remove from oven.

3. Use a pair of tongs to raise the edges of the aluminum foil, tenting it around the roast, so that as it cools, the roast is sitting in the basting liquid and pan juices. Let cool to warm before slicing. Serve with soba noodles prepared with a peanut-garlic sauce.

YIELD: 6 SERVINGS
PAIRING: DRY ASIAN LAGER

# PEPPER FLANK STEAK WITH CHILI-BEER SAUCE

*The sweetness of sun-dried tomatoes reduces the acidity of a potent dark ale such as stout—but they are difficult to chop, even with the sharpest knife. The easiest way to cut the tomatoes into pieces is to trim them into strips with a pair of kitchen shears.*

2 tablespoons minced red bell pepper

½ cup minced onion

2 cloves garlic, minced

5–6 sun-dried tomatoes, snipped into strips

1 tablespoon olive oil

1 cup sweet stout

1 cup chili sauce

1 tablespoon grated horseradish

2 ½–3 pounds flank steak, coated with cracked black pepper and pan-seared to desired degree of doneness

1. Sauté the pepper, onion, garlic, and sun-dried tomatoes in the olive oil in a nonreactive saucepan placed over medium heat. When the vegetables are tender, add the stout and chili sauce, simmer for 5 minutes, and stir in the horseradish.

2. Slice the steak against the grain, on the diagonal, into thin strips. Serve with the sauce on the side.

**YIELD: 4 SERVINGS**
**PAIRING: CRISP, MALTY PILSNER**

# HAM WITH ALE MUSTARD SAUCE

*Deb Carey, president of New Glarus Brewing Company, New Glarus, Wisconsin, makes her Easter ham with a tart Belgian Red cherry ale. I adapted her recipe to include cranberries, whose natural pectin results in a thick sauce. Use sauce made from fresh cranberries instead of canned sauce if possible, and you will have a tart, refreshing fruit and mustard sauce with a lovely reddish color for your ham.*

1½–2 pounds ham steak

½ cup cranberry sauce

1 cup cranberry or cherry ale

2 tablespoons brown sugar

½ teaspoon ground cloves

1 tablespoon powdered mustard

2 tablespoons melted butter

1. Trim ham of any casing or tough, fatty skin and place in a baking dish. Preheat the oven to 325°F.

2. Place the cranberry sauce, fruit ale, brown sugar, cloves, powdered mustard, and melted butter in a blender and mix on high speed until smooth. Pour the mixture into a heavy 1-quart saucepan placed over medium heat and bring to a simmer. Reduce heat and stir until the sugar is melted.

3. Pour the ale sauce over the ham steak and bake for 45 minutes, or until the sauce is slightly browned and bubbly. Serve with a spicy braised cabbage and baked potatoes.

YIELD: 4–6 SERVINGS
PAIRING: TART CHERRY ALE

# PRETZEL-CRUSTED
# PORK LOIN

*Scott McGlinchey, the talented chef and owner of Heaven City, Mukwanago, Wisconsin, introduced me to the idea of using pretzel crumbs in a crust. He uses it for a savory cheesecake, but I find it also makes a great breading to seal in the juices of roasted meats. Pork tenderloins bake quickly, and can dry out. The pretzel coating used here makes the roast moist and flavorful.*

1 cup light North American lager
1 egg
Unsalted pretzel nuggets (to make 2 cups crumbs)
2 tablespoons finely minced scallions
1 teaspoon cracked black pepper
2 pounds pork tenderloin (several pieces)

1. Blend the lager and egg until smooth and place in a long, narrow loaf pan. Set aside.

2. Crush unsalted pretzel nuggets with a rolling pin or in a food processor to make a coarse flour. Set aside.

3. Preheat the oven to 350°F. Blend the scallions and black pepper with the pretzel crumbs in a long, shallow dish. Line a baking sheet with aluminum foil or parchment paper. Roll each tenderloin in the egglager mixture, then in the pretzel crumb blend, and place on the lined baking sheet. Repeat until all the meat is covered with the seasoned pretzel blend.

4. Bake for 30–40 minutes, or until done. Serve sliced thin with spicy mustard and buttered noodles.

YIELD: 4 SERVINGS
PAIRING: MALTY, DARK LAGER

# PAN-SEARED STEAK WITH BOCK BEER MUSHROOM SAUCE

*The marinade for this simple steak recipe calls for roasted garlic, which tastes caramelized and sweeter than raw cloves and thus mellows the bitterness of the beer. The quickest way to roast a handful of garlic cloves is to rub unpeeled cloves with a bit of oil and bake at 300°F in a toaster oven for 10–15 minutes, stirring once or twice to prevent scorching on one side. Or, roast several whole heads of garlic at once, then separate the roasted cloves and double-wrap them in plastic wrap and foil. They will keep in the freezer for several weeks.*

$\frac{1}{4}$ cup bock beer (for marinade)

$\frac{1}{3}$ cup olive oil

5 cloves roasted garlic

3 pounds flank steak

$\frac{1}{4}$ pound oyster mushrooms

$\frac{1}{4}$ pound portabello mushrooms

$\frac{1}{4}$ pound shiitake mushrooms

1 tablespoon olive oil (for sauté)

2 tablespoons finely minced onion

Salt to taste

6 ounces bock beer

1 teaspoon dried thyme

Dash hot pepper sauce

YIELD: 6 SERVINGS
PAIRING: MAIBOCK OR WELL-HOPPED BOCK

1. Blend the ¼ cup beer, the ⅓ cup olive oil, and the roasted garlic in a blender. Place in a gallon-sized zip-seal bag with the flank steak, and refrigerate to marinate.

2. Wash and slice the mushrooms very thin (this can be done in a few seconds, using the 2 mm. slicing blade of a food processor and the wide feed tube).

3. Rub a heavy, nonstick 10-inch saucepan with the 1 tablespoon of olive oil. Place over very low heat and gently sauté the mushrooms, sprinkling with onion and a bit of salt. Stir constantly to prevent sticking, and sauté until the mushrooms are almost dehydrated and crisp.

4. Stir in the 6 ounces of bock and the thyme and let simmer; the mushrooms will absorb the beer and return to tenderness.

5. While the sauce simmers, pan-sear the marinated steak in a heavy skillet set over high heat; a rare steak requires 8–10 minutes per side, while a well-done steak requires 15 minutes per side. Let the steak rest before carving; slice thin, across the grain.

6. Season the mushroom sauce to taste with salt and pepper sauce and serve a spoonful over each thinly sliced portion of steak.

# MINIATURE MEAT LOAVES WITH BOCK BEER

*Bake these miniature meat loaves in muffin cups, and dinner will be ready in minutes. They freeze well, too. To ease chopping sun-dried tomatoes, which can stick to the blade of even the sharpest knife, I use a pair of kitchen shears to snip them into strips, which can then be folded into a dish with ease.*

1 pound lean ground beef

½ pound ground veal

½ pound spicy bulk Italian sausage

1 egg plus 1 egg white

½ cup Italian seasoned bread crumbs (or ½ cup plain bread crumbs with ½ teaspoon each dried parsley and oregano, and pepper to taste)

1 tablespoon minced garlic

½ cup minced onion

½ cup sun-dried tomatoes, snipped with scissors into strips

½ cup bock beer

1. Preheat the oven to 400°F. Place the meat, egg and egg white, bread crumbs, garlic, onion, sun-dried tomatoes, and bock beer in the bowl of a mixer. Use the paddle attachment to stir the ingredients together evenly. You may mix this by hand, but it takes a bit longer to blend evenly, about 5 minutes.

2. Pack into cups of muffin pans (I like to use the large muffin pans). You should have 8 regular-sized muffin

meat loaves, or 6 giant muffin meat loaves. Place the filled muffin pans on foil or a baking sheet to catch drippings as they cook.

3. Place in the oven and reduce heat to 375°F. Bake for 30 minutes, or until the tops are browned and bubbly. The interior will be a bit pink, so cook 10 minutes longer if you prefer well-done meat loaves.

4. Serve with Chili-Beer Sauce (see page 70) or Bock Beer Mushroom Sauce (see page 74).

YIELD: 6–8 SERVINGS
PAIRING: MEDIUM DRY LAGER
OR DORTMUNDER LAGER

# LAMB PATTIES SEARED IN ROSEMARY STOUT

*Fast searing of lamb patties in bread crumbs prior to baking creates a nice crunchy crust and seals in the meat's marinated stout flavor. I save the ends from round loaves of sourdough bread to make fresh bread crumbs; they produce a much tastier crust than do dry crumbs. Begin preparation of this dish the night before; the longer the marinating time, the richer the stout flavor will be in the finished lamb.*

4 ground lamb patties, about 4–5 ounces each
12 ounces sweet stout
2 tablespoons fresh rosemary leaves
Cracked black pepper to taste
2 cups fresh bread crumbs

1. Place lamb patties in a glass 9x9-inch baking dish. Combine the stout and rosemary leaves and pour over the patties. Cover tightly with plastic wrap and let marinate in the refrigerator overnight.

2. Remove the lamb patties from the marinade and strain the reserved liquid through a mesh sieve.

3. Blend the rosemary leaves and pepper with the bread crumbs using a food processor fitted with a metal blade.

4. Preheat the oven to 350°F.

5. Press a layer of the seasoned bread crumbs into both sides of each lamb patty.

6. Place a heavy nonstick skillet over high heat, and sear the lamb patties on both sides, turning after just 3–4 minutes to prevent burning.

7. Place the seared lamb patties on a baking sheet lined with foil. Bake for 20 minutes for lamb patties that are still pink and juicy inside, 30 minutes for well-done lamb. Serve with Cranberry-Rice Pilaf (see page 116).

YIELD: 4 SERVINGS
PAIRING: DRY PORTER

"A glass of bitter beer or pale ale taken with the principal meal of the day, does more good and less harm than any medicine the physicians can prescribe."

Dr. S. Carpenter, 1750

# CHAPTER 6
# SEAFOOD

## ABOUT BEER-BATTERED FISH

"Fish and chips" are the standard fast food of England, washed down with (what else?) a pint of ale. But there are a few tricks to learn when making beer-battered, deep-fried fish at home.

Some recipes for batters advise letting the batter "rest" to prevent toughness (due to gluten formation in the wheat flour). However, the carbonation in beer helps create a light, crispy crust, and beer bubbles do disappear quickly after mixing. Increase the tenderness of the batter by blending some cornstarch or rice flour (which are gluten-free) with the wheat flour, use a highly carbonated beer, and do not over-mix the batter.

To prepare deep-fried seafood to serve six or more people, allow 5 cups vegetable oil, plus 1 cup of peanut oil. Peanut oil is more stable at high temperatures and will help prevent smoking. Use a cooking pot at least twice as large as the measure of oil used for frying; for instance, you would need a 1-gallon pot to accommodate 6 cups of bubbling hot oil safely.

Crispness results from two practices: do not crowd the fish as it cooks (three pieces in a gallon pot is plenty for a single batch) and heat the oil to the correct temperature (370–375°F is ideal). Remember to allow the oil to reheat to this range, as you fry your fish filets in batches. Given these high temperatures, and the risk of burns, use a sturdy, high-sided kettle with a heavy base. It should not tip easily, and must be deep enough to contain several pieces at once, without bubbling over. The frying vessel must be completely dry; even a few drops of water will cause hot oil to splatter.

A few safety pointers: wear hot mitts and use a long pair of tongs to protect your hands as you gently place the fish filets into the oil. The oil will splatter, so clear the stovetop of any other utensils, such as a tea kettle. Prepare a baking sheet lined with paper towels to hold the fried fish and to absorb grease as you remove batches from the hot oil. Keep a large box of baking soda by the stove, should you need to put out any flames.

Choose a dense, white fish that won't fall apart when dipped in batter and fried. The traditional British fish is rock cod; in America good choices would be cod, haddock, whitefish, or scrod. Trim the fish filets into roughly uniform pieces, so that they cook evenly. Pat the cleaned and trimmed fish filets dry between several pieces of paper towel before dipping in the batter. For real British flavor, sprinkle the fried fish, as well as the French-fried potatoes, with a splash of malt vinegar and salt before serving.

Have all your fish prepared and your oil heating up as you make this batter. Use a sieve or slotted spoon to remove any bits of batter floating in the hot oil between batches. This will prevent burnt flavors.

## QUICK BEER BATTER

1 cup flour
$\frac{1}{4}$ cup rice flour or cornstarch
1 egg
$1\frac{1}{4}$ cups amber ale
1 teaspoon salt
$\frac{1}{2}$ teaspoon white pepper
2 pounds firm boneless fish filets, cleaned,
trimmed to roughly uniform size, and patted
dry in paper towels

1. Whisk together the flour and rice flour or cornstarch in a large shallow bowl.

2. In a separate bowl, beat the egg, ale, salt, and pepper together until smooth. Slowly whisk this mixture together with the flour mixture until you have a smooth batter.

3. Dip the prepared filets in the batter, one at a time, and cook in hot oil (370–375°F), in small batches.

4. Allow about 4–7 minutes for each batch, depending on the size and thickness of the fish filets.

5. Use a chopstick, long-handled fork, or tongs to turn the fish filets over as necessary for even cooking. Remove when crust is golden brown.

6. Let the fish drain on paper towels before serving with French fries or potato chips.

YIELD: 4 SERVINGS
PAIRING: CRISP, WELL-HOPPED PALE ALE

# BEER-CRISPED CALAMARI

*These make great appetizers, passed around with a tartar sauce made with capers and lemon.*

2 pounds frozen squid (choose cleaned, fairly small squid or sliced squid rings)
12 ounces light North American lager
1 cup semolina flour (pasta flour)
1 teaspoon salt
$\frac{1}{2}$ teaspoon black pepper
2 tablespoons sweet or hot paprika

1. Rinse the frozen squid in warm water to remove most of the ice; place in a 1-gallon zip-seal plastic bag and pour in the lager. Thaw in the refrigerator overnight, or at room temperature for several hours.

2. When the squid is completely thawed, remove from bag and drain. Do not pat dry. If not already sliced, cut into rings or bite-sized pieces.

3. Prepare the hot oil as described on page 81. Whisk together the semolina flour and seasonings.

4. Dredge the calamari pieces in the flour mixture in batches, and then place in the hot oil. Fry at 375°F for 30–45 seconds or until just golden, stirring with tongs to make sure the pieces cook evenly.

5. Remove from the hot oil with a slotted spoon and let drain for a minute before serving with homemade Caper and Lemon Tartar Sauce. Sprinkle with additional salt and paprika before serving.

## CAPER AND LEMON TARTAR SAUCE

$\frac{1}{2}$ cup light mayonnaise

2 tablespoons minced parsley

1 tablespoon chopped capers

1 clove garlic, crushed

Minced zest from $\frac{1}{2}$ lemon

1 tablespoon Dijon mustard or beer mustard

Salt and pepper to taste

1. Blend all the ingredients in a bowl and chill until ready to serve.

YIELD: 6 SERVINGS AS AN APPETIZER
PAIRING: HONEY WHEAT BEER

# SWORDFISH STEAK SANDWICH

*Terrific for a gourmet picnic or light supper, this sandwich can be assembled in just minutes.*

4 swordfish filets, 1-inch thick
2 tablespoons coarse country mustard
2 tablespoons vegetable oil
$\frac{1}{4}$ cup amber ale
$\frac{1}{4}$ cup minced scallions
1 teaspoon cracked black pepper
20 thin slices cucumber
8 slices hearty cracked wheat bread
Optional: Caper and Lemon Tartar
Sauce (see page 85)

1. Prepare a grill with charcoal. Clean and dry the swordfish filets.

2. Mix the mustard, oil, ale, scallions, and pepper into a seasoned paste. Rub both sides of the swordfish filets with this blend; cover with plastic wrap and refrigerate.

YIELD: 4 SERVINGS
PAIRING: BERLINER WEISSE BEER

3. When the grill is hot and the coals are gray and glowing, place the dressed filets on the grill.

4. Cook about 7–8 minutes on each side. The mustard-scallion paste should char a bit and create an aromatic crust.

5. After cooking is complete, toast the bread briefly on the grill and place swordfish steaks on 4 slices. Cover with thinly sliced cucumber and homemade Caper and Lemon Tartar Sauce, if desired, and the remaining slices of bread. Serve immediately.

# SESAME SALMON STEAKS

*Spicy and nutty salmon steaks complement the nutty, tangy flavors of brown ale. Salmon filets may also be used.*

4 boned salmon steaks (6–8 ounces each)
3 tablespoons tahini (sesame seed paste)
2 tablespoons toasted sesame oil
1 cup nut brown ale
2 tablespoons white sesame seed
1 teaspoon powdered ginger
1 teaspoon cracked black pepper

1. Clean and dry the boned salmon. Mix the tahini, sesame oil, nut brown ale, sesame seed, ginger, and pepper into a marinade. Pour into a gallon-sized zip-seal plastic bag and place the fish inside; seal and refrigerate for at least 8 hours.

2. Prepare a charcoal grill. When the coals are hot, place the marinated salmon filets on the grill. Cook about 7 minutes on each side. Remove from the grill and serve with pasta.

YIELD: 4 SERVINGS
PAIRING: ESB ALE OR DUNKEL WEIZEN

# CORNMEAL CRUST TROUT

*Fresh trout is mild and sweet; use a very light lager to drench the filets before rolling in cornmeal to create a crispy crust that seals in the good flavor.*

1 cup yellow cornmeal
1 teaspoon cracked black pepper
1 teaspoon dill weed
$\frac{1}{2}$ cup light lager
1 egg
6 small filets of trout (4–6 ounces each)
$\frac{1}{4}$ cup butter

1. Whisk together the cornmeal, pepper, and dill weed. Set aside.

2. Beat the lager and egg together and place in a shallow dish. Dredge the cleaned trout filets in lager and egg blend, and then roll gently in cornmeal mixture.

3. Melt the butter in a 10–12-inch heavy skillet placed over medium heat. Pan-fry the trout until tender and flakey, about 10 minutes per inch of thickness, turning halfway through the cooking.

4. Serve with a salad of wild greens and curried rice.

YIELD: 4–6 SERVINGS, DEPENDING ON FILET SIZE
PAIRING: DARK, MALTY LAGER

# SHRIMP POACHED IN BEER

*Norman van Aken, the Florida chef extraordinaire who inspired this recipe, is a fan of beer and seafood, particularly shrimp. To prevent the shrimp from overcooking by absorbing heat from the shells, plunge the cooked shrimp into a bath of ice-cold chili beer. It will preserve the beery, spicy flavors of the shrimp better than a dip into ice water!*

2 quarts water

7 cloves garlic

3 bay leaves

2 tablespoons shrimp boil seasoning (such as Old Bay), or 1 teaspoon each of whole fennel seed, mustard seed, and allspice berries and 1 sprig thyme

3 lemon slices

2 tablespoons salt

24 ounces chili beer, very cold

12 ice cubes

12 ounces dark lager

2 pounds shrimp, 16–20-count medium, with shells and tails attached

YIELD: 8 SERVINGS AS AN APPETIZER
6 SERVINGS AS AN ENTREE
PAIRING: DARK LAGER OR PORTER

1. Place the water, garlic, bay leaves, seasoning blend for shrimp boil, lemon slices, and salt into a 1-gallon stockpot and bring to a boil. Place the chili beer and ice cubes together in a large metal bowl.

2. When the water is boiling vigorously, add the dark lager and the shrimp. Stir well, and let cook for just a few minutes until the shells turn pink.

3. As soon as the shrimp are cooked, remove with a slotted spoon and place in the icy chili beer.

4. When the shrimp are cool enough to touch, remove from the icy beer and place on a platter. Serve with a honey-mustard dipping sauce or horseradish sauce on the side.

"God made yeast,
as well as dough,
and loves fermentation just
as dearly as
he loves vegetation."

Ralph Waldo Emerson

# CHAPTER 7

# VEGETABLE SIDE DISHES

V egetables are among the most challenging of foods to taste with wine, yet they prove to be remarkably beer friendly. In fact, the flavors of the vegetable side dishes presented here are highlighted by the beer styles used as ingredients. The earthy flavor of legumes, natural sweetness of onions, and other vegetables find complements in the malty or spicy flavors present in beer.

The tangy, mineral and acidic flavors of vegetables such as asparagus, spinach, artichokes, and parsnips are naturally enhanced by the flavors of beer. Root vegetables are delicious when braised gently in beer. Some beer aficionados feel that tomatoes are complemented only by robust Vienna-style lagers, due to the relatively high acidity of the fruit.

I think most people eat tomatoes with the addition of so many other spices, herbs, and flavors from sauces and vinaigrettes that the acidic reaction is tempered. Begin your experiments with the beery Welsh Rarebit-baked Tomatoes, and put your own tastebuds to this "acid test." You may be pleased by the gentling effect of the creamy beer cheese sauce on the natural acidity of the sliced baked tomatoes, which are also rendered sweeter by the caramelization that results from baking.

# BAKED TOMATOES WITH WELSH RAREBIT

*This makes a wonderfully colorful side dish to monotone entrées, such as baked fish. The melting cheese sauce transforms even the pale, wan tomatoes sold in winter into a delicious treat. For best results, grate the cheddar when very cold, and then let it warm to room temperature. The cheese will melt more readily.*

2 teaspoons butter

1 tablespoon flour

$\frac{3}{4}$ cup defatted chicken broth

8 ounces grated aged cheddar

1 cup hoppy pale ale, at room temperature

1 teaspoon dried thyme

Several drops hot pepper sauce

1 teaspoon Worcestershire sauce

$\frac{1}{2}$ teaspoon hot mustard powder

4 large tomatoes, cored and sliced into
1-inch-thick rounds

1 tablespoon minced fresh parsley

Salt and pepper to taste

1. Preheat the oven to 350°F. Melt the butter in a heavy 2-quart saucepan over medium heat. Whisk in the flour and cook until golden and toasty, about 3 minutes, whisking steadily. Slowly whisk in the chicken broth and simmer, stirring often, until smooth and thickened. Remove from heat.

2. Let cool for 1 minute, then slowly whisk in handfuls of the cheddar cheese, stirring constantly. Whisk in the ale, thyme, hot pepper sauce, Worcestershire sauce, and mustard powder and return to burner on low heat. Warm through, stirring constantly, to make sure all the cheese is melted. When the cheese is completely melted, remove from heat.

3. Place the tomato slices in the bottom of a large 13x9-inch baking pan. Cover with the Welsh rarebit sauce, sprinkle with parsley and salt and pepper to taste, and bake for 20–25 minutes, or until bubbly.

YIELD: 6 SERVINGS (2 SLICES PER PERSON)

# CARAMELIZED ONION TARTS

*As these yeasty crusts bake, the aromas will remind you of what makes beer "liquid bread."*

## DOUGH

$\frac{1}{4}$ cup warm water

$\frac{1}{2}$ cup amber ale, at room temperature

1 envelope quick-acting yeast

1 tablespoon barley malt syrup or honey

1 cup rye flour

$2\frac{1}{2}$ cups wheat flour

$\frac{1}{4}$ cup vegetable oil (to mix)

1 egg

1 teaspoon salt

1 tablespoon oil (to cover dough)

1. Blend the water and ale with the yeast and malt syrup or honey.

2. Sift the rye and wheat flours into a large mixing bowl.

3. In a separate bowl, whisk together the $\frac{1}{4}$ cup vegetable oil, egg, and salt.

4. Knead together the ale blend, vegetable oil–egg blend, and flour blend. Add more wheat flour, if necessary, to blend the dough into a ball.

5. When the dough is soft, shiny, and well-blended (about 10 minutes by hand, 5 minutes by machine mixer fitted with dough hook), gather into a ball and rub with the 1 tablespoon of oil. Place in an oiled bowl and cover with a damp cloth. Set in a warm spot to rise while preparing the onion filling.

## ONION FILLING

1¼ pounds sweet onions, peeled and sliced very thin

2 tablespoons olive oil

⅔ cup doppelbock or other malty lager

½ teaspoon cracked black pepper

2 tablespoons finely minced fresh parsley

Salt to taste

1. Cut the onion slices into quarters and place in a non-stick skillet with the olive oil. Sauté over low heat, stirring often, until translucent.

2. Stir in the doppelbock, pepper, parsley, and salt to taste. Continue to sauté over low heat until the onion is golden and caramelized but not burnt, about 10 minutes. Remove from heat and set aside.

## ASSEMBLING THE TARTS

1 teaspoon crumbled dried thyme

4 tablespoons grated Parmesan cheese

1. Preheat the oven to 375°F. Line a baking sheet with parchment paper.

2. Sprinkle flour on a clean work surface and divide the dough. Roll each half into a round ball, and then roll evenly into a circle about ¾-inch thick. Roll up the edges of the circle to form a crust. Pinch with fingertips or a fork to crimp the crust into position.

3. Place crusts on the lined baking sheet. Fill each crust with half the caramelized onion mixture.

4. Sprinkle each with ½ teaspoon thyme and 2 tablespoons Parmesan cheese.

5. Bake for 30 minutes, or until the tops are golden.

**YIELD: 8 SERVINGS**

# BAKED LIMA BEANS

4½ cups frozen lima beans, thawed
5 tablespoons butter
3 tablespoons minced garlic
2 cups light sour half-and-half
1 tablespoon dry mustard powder
¼ cup molasses
1 cup brown ale
½ teaspoon salt
1 teaspoon red pepper flakes
½ cup bread crumbs
½ cup minced parsley

1. Place the lima beans in a mesh strainer to drain. Preheat the oven to 400°F. Melt the butter in a small skillet placed over medium heat and add the garlic. Sauté lightly until garlic is golden and butter is browned and bubbly, but do not let the garlic burn. Remove from heat and let cool.

2. Combine all ingredients and pour lima bean mixture into a 2-quart baking dish. Bake 1 hour. Makes a good side dish for a buffet supper.

YIELD: 8 SERVINGS

# CELERY, PEPPERS, AND LAGERED PECANS

1 yellow bell pepper
1 red bell pepper
1 tablespoon olive oil
5–6 stalks celery, sliced
$\frac{1}{2}$ cup pecans
$\frac{1}{3}$ cup Pilsner lager
Optional: Salt, pepper, and/or hot sauce to taste

1. Remove the seeds and slice the bell peppers into thin 1-inch-long strips. Place in the bottom of a heavy nonstick 9- or 10-inch skillet fitted with a tight lid and stir in the olive oil. Sauté over low heat for 2–3 minutes, then add the celery. Cover and let sauté for 5 minutes, stirring occasionally.

2. Toast the pecans in a toaster oven. Place the pecans and lager in a blender and pulse on high speed for half a minute, or until the pecans are chopped but not pulverized.

3. Pour the lager and pecan blend into the skillet, stir well, and taste. Add a little salt, pepper, and/or hot sauce if desired.

YIELD: 4–6 SERVINGS AS A SIDE DISH

# KRIEK RED CABBAGE

*"Kriek" is the Flemish word for cherry, and this easy side dish is made with Belgian-style cherry ale, dried cherries, and thinly sliced red cabbage.*

$\frac{1}{3}$ cup dried sweetened red cherries

1 cup cherry ale or kriek beer

1 tablespoon olive oil

1 teaspoon minced orange zest

1 tablespoon minced shallots or mild sweet onion

10–12 ounces red cabbage, cored,
peeled, and sliced thin

Salt and pepper to taste

1. Place the cherries in an ovenproof dish and cover with the cherry ale or kriek beer. Cover with plastic wrap and place in a microwave. Heat on high power for 1 minute, then remove from oven, remove wrap, and let cool.

2. Stir together the olive oil, orange zest, and shallots or sweet onion in a 10-inch heavy nonstick skillet, placed over low heat. Sauté gently until the shallots or onion are translucent and tender, about 3 minutes.

YIELD: 4 SERVINGS

3. Add the cabbage, cherries, and ale, and sauté, stirring often, for approximately 15 minutes, or until the cabbage is tender.

4. Season to taste with salt and pepper and serve with roast poultry or roast pork.

# ARTICHOKES WITH LEMON LAGER SAUCE

*Artichokes are great when dipped into this mock hollandaise sauce. It is made with a whole egg and browned butter for rich flavor without as much fat and cholesterol as the traditional yolks-only sauce.*

4 artichokes
1 gallon boiling water
1 egg
½ cup Pilsner lager
1 teaspoon cornstarch
1 tablespoon fresh lemon juice
Pinch cayenne pepper
2 tablespoons butter

1. Trim the long stems and tough outer leaves from the artichokes. Use a pair of tongs to put the artichokes into the boiling water and let cook until tender, about 35–45 minutes, depending on size.

2. Place the egg, lager, cornstarch, lemon juice, and cayenne pepper in a blender, cover the lid with a towel, and hold down to prevent splashes. The lager will foam quite a bit.

3. Melt the butter in a 1-quart heavy saucepan over very low heat until deep gold; the milk solids will foam up and turn brown. Skim off the browned bits and, whisking continuously, add the lager-lemon mixture.

4. Cook the sauce over low heat, whisking constantly, until it thickens. Serve warm, as a dipping sauce for the artichokes.

YIELD: 4 SERVINGS, 2–3 TABLESPOONS
PER SERVING

# TWICE-BAKED POTATOES

*These giant potatoes gain the flavor of pale ale through two steps: baking, followed by mashing with cheese and ale. By cutting the potatoes in half, you halve the baking time, too.*

6 Idaho baking potatoes, 10–12 ounces each

3 tablespoons snipped fresh chives

$1\frac{2}{3}$ cups pale ale

8 ounces light cream cheese (neufchatel)

2 ounces minced crisp cooked bacon

$\frac{1}{3}$ cup minced parsley

$\frac{1}{4}$ cup minced scallions

Salt and pepper to taste

1. Preheat the oven to 400°F. Scrub and slice the baking potatoes in half lengthwise. Place sliced-side down on a large, deep-rimmed baking sheet, and pour in $1\frac{1}{3}$ cups of the pale ale. Place the pan in the oven and bake until the potatoes are fork tender, about 35–45 minutes.

YIELD: 8 SERVINGS

2. Remove the potatoes from the oven and let cool 15 minutes. Use a hot mitt to pick up each potato half and scoop out the still-warm contents into a bowl. Be sure not to puncture the skins. Set the empty skins aside.

3. Mash the warm potatoes with the remaining $\frac{1}{3}$ cup pale ale, cream cheese, bacon, parsley, scallions, and salt and pepper to taste. Use a mixing paddle on a standing mixer or a masher to blend (avoid using a food processor, which produces gummy, soupy potatoes).

4. Pack the mashed potato blend back into 8 of the skins. Discard remaining skins. You may cover and refrigerate the potatoes for up to 12 hours; return to a 400°F oven and warm through before serving.

"I lived from bread of black wheat, and drank from beer of white wheat."

Ancient Egyptian Funeral Inscription

# CHAPTER 8
## BREADS AND GRAINS

Great grains and pilafs can be prepared with beer. The natural bready flavors from the malts used to brew beer make excellent accents for a wide range of savory breads, muffins, and grain dishes. Still, few people make a meal of bread alone; they add lots of sliced cheeses, spicy mustards, deli meats, and more for sandwich fixings. Thus, no beer pairings are suggested for the breads, except for a few sweet breads that could stand in for dessert.

Remember that yeast bread baked with beer often rises a bit more than bread baked with water. That is because the sugars in the beer feed the yeast and increase its leavening power. Use a generously sized loaf pan to accommodate the extra heft of the dough.

# BUTTERY BEER CROUTONS

*Credit for the idea of beery croutons goes to HOPS!Bistro and Brewery, a chain of brewpubs that serve a similar version of these toasted bread slices as the base for several appetizers. The croutons are tasty with all kinds of dips and spreads, or may accompany a French onion soup.*

4 ounces butter (1 stick)
$\frac{1}{2}$ cup wheat beer
$\frac{1}{3}$ cup freshly grated Parmesan cheese
1 egg
2 tablespoons roughly chopped parsley
4 cloves roasted garlic (see page 74)
Salt and pepper to taste
16 slices baguette bread

1. Brown the butter in a 9-inch heavy skillet placed over medium heat. Remove from heat when the butter starts to foam and turn light brown. Set aside to cool. Strain through a fine-mesh sieve when cool but still liquid, to remove browned bits of milk proteins.

2. Place the strained butter, wheat beer, Parmesan cheese, egg, parsley, roasted garlic, and salt and pepper to taste in a food processor fitted with a metal blade. Process on high speed for several minutes or until the mixture is smooth and emulsified. Scrape into a container fitted with a tight lid. Seal and chill until the mixture is solid.

3. Preheat the oven to 325°F. Spread rounds of baguettes with the chilled butter-cheese mixture, place on a baking sheet, and toast until golden brown and bubbly. Serve with soups, salads, dips, or deli meats.

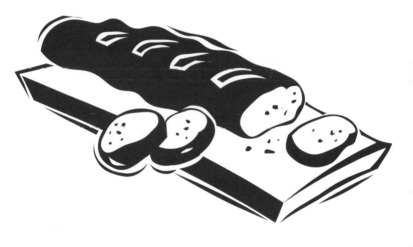

YIELD: 16 CROUTONS

# STEELHEAD BREAD

*Teri Fahrendorf, head brewer of the Steelhead Brewery in Eugene, Oregon, is an avid baker. I developed this recipe, patterned after one she described in an interview in* The Celebrator, *a beer magazine.*

1 tablespoon active dry yeast

1½ cups amber or brown ale, warmed to 70°F

2 tablespoons dark barley malt syrup
or buckwheat honey

2 tablespoons vegetable oil

1¼ cups steel cut oats

½ cup malted milk powder

1½ cups millet flour

1 teaspoon salt

2 cups bread flour

1 teaspoon oil (to cover dough)


1. Dissolve the yeast in the ale. Whisk in the malt syrup or honey and the 2 tablespoons vegetable oil.

2. Place the oats in a blender or food processor fitted with a metal blade and grind into a coarse flour (about 1–2 minutes on high speed).

3. Stir together the malted milk powder, millet flour, oats, salt, and bread flour. Knead in the wet ingredients and knead until the dough is elastic and shiny. Rub the dough with 1 teaspoon oil and place in a greased bowl.

4. Cover with a damp tea towel and leave to rise in a warm spot on top of the oven. After 1 hour, punch down the dough, form a loaf shape, and let rise for another $1\frac{1}{4}$ hours. Preheat the oven to 350°F and bake for 50–60 minutes.

YIELD: 1 LOAF, 12–15 SLICES

# KRIEK CHERRY MUFFINS

*Start preparations for these muffins the night before, by soaking the dried cherries in the ale overnight. The result is a deeper fruited ale flavor.*

½ cup dried cherries

1 cup Belgian-style kriek or cherry ale

½ cup butter, softened

1 cup sugar

1 egg, at room temperature

1½ cups flour

½ teaspoon baking soda

1 teaspoon baking powder

½ teaspoon salt

½ cup ground almonds

1. Preheat the oven to 375°F and grease two 6-cup muffin tins, or a 24-cup miniature muffin tin. If you have not been able to plump the cherries in the ale overnight, here is a shortcut: place the cherries in an ovenproof glass dish, cover with ale, and seal with plastic wrap. Microwave on high power for 1 minute, remove wrap, and let cherries cool.

2. Cream the butter and sugar together in a 4-quart mixing bowl, then beat in the egg. Beat until fluffy. Drain the cherries, but reserve the fruited ale.

3. Stir together the flour, baking soda, baking powder, salt, and ground almonds. Stir into the butter-sugar mixture, then add the drained cherries and 2 table-spoons of the reserved fruited ale.

4. Fill the muffin cups ⅔ full with the batter. Bake for 20–35 minutes, depending on the size of the muffin cups. The muffins should be lightly browned on top. Apply Syrup Glaze as described below.

### SYRUP GLAZE

2 tablespoons butter
2 tablespoons sugar
Remaining fruited ale

1. Melt the butter, sugar, and the remaining fruited ale in a small saucepan over low heat until the sugar is dissolved. Lightly brush the hot muffins with the glaze and allow to cool. The glaze will help keep the muffins moist for several days.

YIELD: 12–24 MUFFINS

# COUNTRY HAM BISCUITS

*Southern country hams tend to be salty, so I've left out the salt in this biscuit recipe. By using self-rising flour, you save a step in mixing. These biscuits can be ready for brunch in 20 minutes.*

1 cup light North American lager
2 cups self-rising flour
2 tablespoons melted butter
½ cup diced cooked country ham
Milk

1. Preheat the oven to 425°F. Place all the ingredients (except the milk) in the bowl of a food processor fitted with a metal blade. Pulse to mix; just 4–5 short pulses should moisten and combine all ingredients. Do not overmix.

2. Line a baking sheet with parchment paper. Drop batter from a tablespoon onto the sheet. Brush the tops of the biscuits with milk.

3. Bake for 12–15 minutes, or until the biscuits are golden brown on top. Serve with brunch dishes such as omelets.

YIELD: 2 DOZEN SMALL BISCUITS
PAIRING: DUNKEL WEIZEN

# MALTED BARLEY PILAF

*The chewy texture of pearl barley makes this a substantial side dish.*

2 tablespoons olive oil
1 cup pearl barley
$\frac{3}{4}$ cup defatted chicken broth
$1\frac{1}{4}$ cups water
1 teaspoon salt
$\frac{1}{2}$ cup currants
$\frac{3}{4}$ cup Scotch ale
1 cup chopped pecans
1 cup chopped scallions (green parts as well)

1. Place the olive oil and barley in a heavy 10-inch nonstick skillet with a lid, placed over medium heat. Toast the barley in the oil until it turns light gold. Pour in the chicken broth and $\frac{3}{4}$ cup of the water; bring to a simmer. Add the salt, stir, and cover. Add more water as the cooking liquid is absorbed by the grain.

2. Place the currants and Scotch ale in an ovenproof glass dish and cover with plastic wrap. Microwave on high heat for 1 minute, remove wrap, and let fruit cool in the ale.

3. Toast the pecans in an 8-inch skillet set over low heat. When the barley is tender, remove from heat. Stir in the currants and ale, toasted pecans, and scallions. Serve as a side dish for lamb patties or other roasted meats.

YIELD: 4 SERVINGS AS A SIDE DISH

# CRANBERRY-RICE PILAF

*The sour taste of dried cranberries is balanced by the sweetness of sautéed onions in this easy pilaf.*

½ cup dried cranberries

1 cup cranberry or cherry ale

1 tablespoon olive oil

⅓ cup diced onion

⅓ cup orzo

2 cups water

1 cup rice

1 tablespoon butter

½ cup minced celery

½ cup minced fresh parsley

Salt and pepper to taste

Optional garnish: 2 tablespoons toasted pine nuts

1. Macerate the dried cranberries in the fruit ale overnight.

2. Place the olive oil, onion, and orzo in a heavy, non-stick skillet and slowly sauté over very low heat. The onions will turn golden (keep the heat low and watch to prevent burning at the edges), while the orzo will be toasted.

**YIELD: 4 SERVINGS AS A SIDE DISH**

3. Meanwhile, bring the water to a boil in a 1-quart saucepan fitted with a lid. Sprinkle in the rice and butter when the water is boiling rapidly, stir and reduce heat, cover, and cook until the water is absorbed, about 20 minutes.

4. Add the plumped fruit and remaining ale to the skillet, cover, and cook over low heat; the orzo should steam and absorb the fruited ale's flavor. Stir occasionally to prevent sticking; add more ale if necessary to simmer the orzo to tenderness.

5. Stir the celery and parsley into the skillet when both the rice and orzo are fully cooked and tender; then add the rice to the skillet. Stir well to mix, season with salt and pepper, and sprinkle toasted pine nuts on top if you wish. Serve with grilled meat or fish.

"There are more old drunks
than old doctors."

Anonymous

# CHAPTER 9
## DESSERTS

From the delicate pink hue of a classic frambozen (or raspberry wheat beer) to the deep
espresso color of a dark chocolate stout, the
rich flavors of beer can complement or contrast
with the sweetness of many desserts. Just as liqueurs
and extracts add another layer of flavor to dessert
recipes, so, too, does beer add another dimension of
taste. Its subtle hops bitterness balances the unctuous sweetness of honey, vanilla, or even creamy white chocolate. Enjoy
the interplay of flavors between a full range of bold-flavored
beers and sweets, from the simplest "portered" molasses
cookies to an elaborate sundae of malted white chocolate
brownies with mocha stout frozen custard.

# CHOCOLATE MALT WAFFLES

*Whip up a batch of these waffles for a midnight snack or a brunch dish. Excellent with sliced fresh strawberries and chopped pecans as a garnish.*

2 eggs

1 cup malty lager

$\frac{2}{3}$ cup sugar

$\frac{1}{4}$ cup unsweetened cocoa powder

$\frac{1}{4}$ cup malted milk powder (you may substitute Ovaltine)

$1\frac{1}{2}$ cups flour

2 teaspoons baking powder

$\frac{1}{2}$ teaspoon salt

4 tablespoons butter

2 ounces bittersweet chocolate, chopped

Cooking oil spray

1. Preheat a waffle iron. Blend the eggs and lager.

2. Sift together the sugar, cocoa, malted milk powder, flour, baking powder, and salt.

3. Blend the wet and dry ingredients in a large mixing bowl until just combined; the batter will be lumpy.

4. Melt together the butter and chocolate in a glass measuring cup set in the microwave and covered loosely with plastic wrap (butter sometimes erupts in the microwave). Heat on high for 1 minute, stir, then return to heat for another 30–40 seconds.

5. Use a fork to stir the melted butter and chocolate until warm, not hot. Blend the butter-chocolate mixture into the batter.

6. Spritz the waffle iron griddle with cooking oil spray and place $\frac{1}{3} - \frac{1}{2}$ cup batter in the center. Use a spatula to spread it slightly, then cook according to the waffle iron manufacturer's instructions. About 2–3 minutes is the usual cooking time for a 6-inch Belgian style waffle (or until steam is no longer visible from the sides of the closed waffle iron).

YIELD: 6–8 WAFFLES
PAIRING: PORTER, EXTRA STOUT,
OR A DRY, SPICY WIT BEER

# PEACH LAMBIC ICE CREAM

*Charles Finkel of Merchant du Vin, Seattle, sponsors many beer dinners across the United States. At one event in Scottsdale, Arizona, the chef at the Phoenician Resort devised a raspberry sorbet made from Lindemans framboise, or raspberry beer. His creation inspired me to try the following creamy dessert confection—with peaches. Vanilla syrup (Monin and Torani are brand names) may be found at gourmet food stores and specialty coffee shops such as Coffee Connection, Gloria Jean's Coffee Bean, and Starbucks.*

1½ cups peach purée (see note below)

½ cup sugar

1 cup peach lambic

1 envelope (2 teaspoons) unflavored gelatin, softened in 3 tablespoons warm water

1 cup heavy cream

½ cup vanilla syrup

Ice cream machine

Garnish: sliced carambola (star fruit)

1. Blend the peach purée, sugar, and lambic. Cover and chill in the refrigerator overnight.

2. Remove the fruit blend from the refrigerator and warm to room temperature. Blend the softened gelatin with the fruit-beer mixture, then fold in the heavy cream and vanilla syrup.

3. Cover the mixture and chill well. Scrape into an ice cream machine and freeze according to manufacturer's instructions. Garnish with the star fruit.

NOTE: Peach purée is made from peeled, pitted peaches, cooked with 3 tablespoons of sugar to every 1 cup of fruit. The cooked fruit is then puréed in a food mill or food processor until it becomes a thick sauce.

YIELD: 1 SCANT QUART
PAIRING: APRICOT OR PEACH ALE

# PORTER MOLASSES COOKIES

*Michael Horne, a beer critic, suggested making a molasses cookie with porter. After several batches and taste tests, these recipes won my approval (and that of a few willing taste testers).*

½ cup butter

⅔ cup brown sugar

1 egg, at room temperature

¾ cup dark molasses

1 teaspoon vanilla extract

½ teaspoon ground cinnamon

1 teaspoon powdered ginger

1 teaspoon baking soda

2 ¼ cups flour

¼ cup sour cream

⅔ cup porter, at room temperature

1 cup granulated sugar

Optional glaze: 1 tablespoon each of porter and cream, blended with ⅓ cup confectioner's sugar

1. Cream the butter and brown sugar together until smooth and emulsified, then add the egg and beat until fluffy. Pour in the molasses and vanilla extract. Blend well.

2. Sift together the cinnamon, ginger, baking soda, and flour. Place the sour cream and porter in a large bowl and whisk together.

3. Add the sifted dry ingredients, alternating with the sour cream–porter blend, to the butter mixture, beating continuously. The batter will be soft. Preheat the oven to 350°F.

4. Chill the batter for 15 minutes to stiffen it. Drop golf ball–sized mounds of dough from a tablespoon into a large shallow bowl of granulated sugar. Dust each ball of dough in the sugar, then place on a parchment-lined baking sheet. Repeat with successive spoonfuls of dough until two baking sheets are filled (about 3 dozen cookies). Flatten the cookies slightly with the base of a small glass dipped in sugar.

5. Bake for 15–20 minutes, or until golden brown and puffy. Glaze the cookies if you wish. They will keep in a sealed container for up to 1 week.

YIELD: APPROXIMATELY 3 DOZEN 3-INCH-
DIAMETER COOKIES
PAIRING: PORTER OR BROWN ALE

# MALTED WHITE CHOCOLATE BROWNIES

*The original inspiration for these white chocolate brownies came from Karen Barker, co-owner and pastry chef of the Magnolia Grill in Durham, North Carolina. I adapted her recipe by reducing the amount of butter and adding both lager and malted milk powder to the batter. The result is a more cakelike brownie with a slight lemony tang from the hops in the lager.*

10 ounces white chocolate (see note below)
½ cup butter (1 stick)
3 eggs
¾ cup sugar
¼ teaspoon salt
¾ teaspoon vanilla extract
1½ cups flour
⅓ cup malted milk powder
½ cup crisp, well-hopped lager, at room temperature
Chocolate Malt Ganache (see recipe below)

1. Preheat the oven to 350°F. Butter an 11½x16½-inch jelly roll pan. Line it with parchment paper. Butter and flour the paper.

2. Put the chocolate and butter in a glass dish loosely covered with plastic wrap and place in a microwave. Melt on high for 1 minute, stir, heat on high again for another minute, then remove from microwave. Allow to cool.

3. In a 4-quart mixing bowl, whip the eggs with the sugar and salt until very thick and light, about 5–8 minutes. Add the vanilla.

4. Whisk in the melted chocolate mixture. Sift the flour and malted milk powder together over the mixing bowl. Fold in the flour blend gently, alternating with the lager beer.

5. Spread the batter in the prepared pan and bake for approximately 25–30 minutes, or until the top is evenly browned.

NOTE: Do not substitute white confectionery coating for the white chocolate; real white chocolate has less sugar and is higher in cocoa fat, so it will melt properly and will not burn in the oven. The white confectionery coating is often high in sugar, corn syrup, and emulsifiers, which produces a chalky texture and too-rapid browning.

## CHOCOLATE MALT GANACHE

*Briess Malting Company, Chilton, Wisconsin, is one of the few remaining producers of specialty malts in North America and also makes a concentrated brewer's wort (CBW), or liquid extract produced from malted barley. The Traditional Dark CBW accentuates the chocolate flavor in this creamy ganache frosting.*

3 ounces semisweet chocolate
$\frac{1}{4}$ cup heavy cream
2 tablespoons dark malt extract syrup (sold through homebrew supply shops)
3 tablespoons confectioner's sugar

1. Melt the chocolate and stir in the cream and dark malt extract syrup. Beat on high speed until fluffy, then gradually add confectioner's sugar to make a thicker frosting. Frost the brownies after they have cooled.

YIELD: 2 DOZEN 2-INCH-SQUARE BROWNIES
PAIRING: SWEET STOUT

# PORTERED CHOCOLATE PUDDING

*These little custardy treats get a luscious espresso-roast aftertaste from the addition of porter.*

1 teaspoon cornstarch

$\frac{1}{2}$ cup half-and-half

$\frac{1}{2}$ cup plus 1 tablespoon sugar

5 ounces bittersweet chocolate, chopped

3 eggs

$\frac{2}{3}$ cup porter

1. Blend the cornstarch, half-and-half, $\frac{1}{2}$ cup sugar, and chopped chocolate in a heavy nonstick 1-quart saucepan. Place over low heat and stir until the sugar and chocolate melt. Remove from heat and let cool 1 minute.

2. Beat the eggs and porter together until frothy.

3. Stir the egg-porter mixture into the chocolate base and set over low heat. Whisk constantly, until the pudding thickens. For a perfectly smooth pudding, strain the mixture. Pour into custard cups and let cool at room temperature, then chill. Dust with the 1 tablespoon of sugar before serving.

YIELD: 6 SERVINGS
PAIRING: CHERRY ALE OR RASPBERRY LAMBIC

# BIRRA MISU

*The Italians call the traditional dessert of ladyfinger sponge cakes soaked in espresso and topped with creamy mascarpone cheese a "tirami-su." Several brewpubs, such as HOPS!Bistro and Brewery and Phoenix Brewing Co., have experimented with beer in tirami-su, substituting a strong ale for the espresso. My version uses a potent barleywine to augment strong coffee and coffee-flecked chocolate.*

8 ladyfingers

1 cup barleywine

$\frac{1}{4}$ cup espresso

$\frac{1}{4}$ cup sugar

2 tablespoons coffee liqueur

$\frac{1}{2}$ cup heavy cream

1 cup mascarpone cheese

1 cup grated chocolate (try the espresso-flavored Tropical Source chocolate from Cloud Nine)

1. Slice ladyfingers in half and place bottom layers in a shallow 6x10-inch serving dish. Cakes should fit snugly into dish.

2. Mix the barleywine, espresso, 1 tablespoon of the sugar, and the coffee liqueur in a 2-cup measure, stirring well until the sugar is dissolved. Drizzle about half of this blend over the ladyfingers.

3. In a 1-quart bowl, whip cream and remaining sugar until soft peaks form. Whip in mascarpone. Spread 2 tablespoons of blend on each ladyfinger. Top with 1–2 teaspoons of chocolate. Place tops on ladyfingers to make a "sandwich," drizzle with remaining barleywine mixture, and garnish with remaining cream-cheese blend and grated chocolate. Chill 1–2 hours before serving. May be held 24 hours before serving.

YIELD: 8 SERVINGS (1 LADYFINGER PER PORTION)
PAIRING: SWEET STOUT

"Beer that is not drunk has
missed its vocation"

Meyer Breslau, 1880

## CHAPTER 10
# AFTER DINNER

S tretch out the pleasure of company by serving after-dinner treats. From sophisticated beers that are potent enough to supplant brandy or liqueurs, to pairings of ale and cheese that make a great after-theatre snack, there are many ways to enjoy beer as night draws to a close.

## BARLEYWINES AND DESSERT BEERS

Barleywines and dessert beers are characterized by more robust flavors, higher alcohol content, and, occasionally, the use of additional spices, herbs, berries, and unusual barley malts. You might try the Dunkel Weizen Barleywine from Colorado's Odells Brewing Co., the elegant smoothness of Bigfoot Barleywine from California's Sierra Nevada Brewing, or the aromatic Holiday Spice Lager from Wisconsin's Lakefront Brewery—to name just a few of the many fine dessert brews available.

The Belgians have an affinity for strong ales: a seasonal specialty, the NOEL Christmas Ale from Affligem Abbey, has the velvety rich mouthfeel and higher-than-average alcohol content that typifies barleywines. It is slightly sweet and presents some roasty notes like cocoa bean from the extravagant use of dark malts. Bush Noel, another seasonal strong Belgian ale, tastes almost spicy and peppery, thanks to its high alcohol content.

San Francisco's Anchor Brewing releases a slightly different version of its special strong ale each year; the 1995 ale was notable for its great balance and complex aroma, with just hints of spice melded into the piney hops perfume.

Samichlaus dark lager from Brauerei Hurlimann of Zurich, brewed but once a year, is released close to

Thanksgiving in the U.S. It is as potent as a barleywine: its alcohol strength exceeds that of many wines. It is syrupy, with hints of treacle and brandy on the palate, and makes an excellent companion to rich chocolate desserts.

Other styles of beer, such as Scotch ales and fruit ales, also make ideal dessert beers. A richly fruity cherry beer from Wisconsin's New Glarus Brewing, Belgian Red Ale, makes a delightful complement to a fruit tart, while the creamy sweetness of the White Chocolate Malted Brownies could be paired with a contrasting toffee flavor from a deep stout.

Base your after-dinner beer choices on other brews sampled during the course of an evening, as well as seasonal influences. A lightly citric weiss beer might taste very refreshing after an evening spent sampling sweet, malty lagers, particularly if the weather is warm. A wee dram of McEwan's Scotch Ale might be preferable in the middle of winter.

## CHEESES AND BEER

A typical Belgian bar snack consists of a fresh soft farmer's cheese, not quite as rich as mascarpone, spread on bread with slices of mild radish. And in England, the ploughman's lunch consists of bread, fruit, cheese, and ale. Cheese and beer have long been recognized as partners on the palate.

But good cheese and beer combinations go beyond the classic cheddar and ale ploughman's pairing, to unexpected delights. For example, a benefit beer tasting organized by the Wisconsin Milk Marketing Board for an American Cheese Society meeting in Green Bay, Wisconsin, showed that Belgian fruit ales go very well with rind-ripened cheeses. The lambic ale known as kriek (cherry in Flemish) is brewed with wild yeasts and infused with both delightful color and bouquet from the addition of fresh, sour cherries during aging. The fruity, sweet-sour taste of the beer pairs well with the buttery or earthy flavors of ripened brie. Brie's flavor ranges from mild to pungent, depending on its age.

Maibock is brewed to celebrate the first warm days of spring, with plenty of refreshingly bitter hops, which pairs well with the nutty flavors of gruyère, a firm, hearty cheese. Gruyère is the traditional cheese for fondue, which may be prepared with strong ale instead of white wine.

Red ales or deep amber ales complement the complex character and zesty flavor of parmesan. Parmesan's sweet, somewhat buttery and nutty flavor profile, and its crumbly, granular texture make it a fine ingredient in dishes prepared with beer. Another favorite cheese and beer pairing is the piquant flavor of gorgonzola matched with oatmeal stout, an ale full of toasty malt flavor. A balanced stout provides a nicely carbonated contrast to the creaminess of the cheese.

When tasting cheese, be sure to progress from mild, buttery fresh cheeses, to the sharper aged or mold-ripened cheeses such as cheddar and gorgonzola. Cheese slices most easily when cold, but tastes best when served at room temperature. Thus, slice the cheese as soon as it emerges from the refrigerator, but cover with plastic wrap and permit it to warm up a bit before tasting.

Taste rind-washed or ripened cheeses both with and without the rind; sometimes the enzymes present in the mold will interact unpleasantly with the bitterness in beer. It is very easy to trim even a soft-ripened cheese such as brie or camembert, by using a cheese wire or a length of sanitized wire. Or, you can use a thin, long serrated knife that has been lightly oiled to prevent the cheese from sticking.

After opening a piece of cheese from a plastic package, be sure to use fresh plastic wrap to seal it for storage. Reusing old wrappings, or wrapping cheese in foil, hastens the spoilage of the cheese.

## CHOCOLATE AND BEER

It could be called bitter-sweet: a malty beer with a sweet chocolate dessert makes a decadent duo.

Chocolate desserts, from creamy pâtés, flourless tortes, and buttery truffles, can prove to be too palate-coating and heavy for a delicate dessert wine. However, the robust roasted flavors of dark ales and lagers match the intensity of dark cocoa and chocolate confections.

In fact, one British brewer, Whitbread, created a special mild ale called Fuggles Chocolate. Its secret ingredients? None other than cocoa extract and dark roasted barley known as chocolate malt (so called for its color, not because it is made with cocoa beans).

As an historical aside, crushed cocoa beans were used to flavor dark ales in England in the 1600s, before hops were commercially available.

The F.X. Matt's Saranac Chocolate Amber Lager,

Mackeson's Stout, Desnoes and Geddes Dragon Stout, and Murphy's Irish Stout all derive much of their full-bodied character from the chocolate and black malts. Scottish ales, such as Belhaven or Caledonian MacAndrews, also complement a chocolate dessert through their gentle bitterness and soft, full malt flavors. A Scottish ale brewed by Chris Johnson of Swan's Buckerfield Brewery in Victoria, B.C., was so chocolatey that beer critic Steve Beaumont dubbed it "the Count Chocula of brews."

Taste a variety of dark beers with samples of good quality, bittersweet chocolate. You may be amazed and delighted by the flavors they both accentuate.

# APPENDICES

## BEER-TASTING MENUS

Here are two sample menus for beer tasting events, featuring recipes and pairing recommendations from this book. Several items, such as the Artichoke and Cheese Dip, Chicken Tenders, Sesame Spinach Salad, and Cranberry-Rice Pilaf, may be made up to 24 hours in advance to streamline your party planning.

### TASTING FOR 20

Artichoke and Cheese Dip—strong pale ale or Belgian wit
Pork Satay with Peanut Ale Sauce—dry Asian lager
Steak Salad with Dunkel Rye Croutons—dunkel weizen
Chicken Tenders with Coffee Stout Glaze—
malty lager or kölsch
Porter Chili-Paste Grilled Shrimp—amber ale
or Trappist ale

### DINNER FOR 6

Beer-Crisped Calamari—honey weiss ale
Sesame Spinach Salad—robust pale ale
Lamb Seared with Rosemary Stout with side of
Cranberry-Rice Pilaf—dry porter
Malted White Chocolate Brownies—triple stout

### PLANNING A BEER TASTING

Choose the beer selection according to your guests' tastes and your budget; a tasting of domestic bock lagers will be less expensive than a selection of imported Belgian fruit ales.

Purchase the beer from a reliable retailer, so you can be sure to have fresh beer in top condition to serve to your guests. Serve it at the optimum temperature.

When planning the order of a tasting that presents a spectrum of styles, begin with the lightest, least bitter, and lowest in alcohol beers. Progress to the beers that are darker, more bitter, and higher in alcohol content. Pay the most attention to the hoppiness or bitterness of the beer. Extremely acidic and highly hopped beers, even those that are light in color, will eclipse other flavors in darker but milder-tasting beers that follow in your tasting.

Plan to serve 3-4 ounces of each beer; for a tasting of six to eight brews this works out to approximately two bottles of beer per person. Spread over two to three hours, that rate of consumption should prevent intoxication unless the beers to be tasted are high in alcohol. Pour smaller samples of strong ales, bocks, doppelbocks, winter warmers, barleywines, and other relatively high alcohol brews.

You may use small, straight-sided 5-ounce juice glasses, 8-ounce all-purpose beverage glasses, or even wine glasses; but note that the larger the glass, the less likely you are to be able to enjoy all the aromas in a single sniff. Whatever style of glass you choose, make sure it is clean and dust-free.

Provide appropriate foods and water to cleanse the palate. Breads or crackers (preferably unsalted and unseasoned) can serve the purpose. Be aware that cheeses coat the palate, and will alter the perception of the beers tasted with them. However, if your tasting is very informal, a platter of mild cheeses and crackers is a simple accompaniment.

Give guests a chance to learn about the breweries that produce the beers. Get a little background information on the breweries from local distributors or on-line information sources. Sources such as *Beer Across America* by Marty Nachel (Storey Publishing, 1995), *The Encyclopedia of Beer* (Henry Holt, 1995), *The Ultimate Beer Encyclopedia* by Roger Protz (in the USA, distributed by Chatauqua Press) or *The Ultimate Book of Beer Trivia* (Bluewood Books, 1994), also contain fun facts that give drinkers a new perspective on the beer in their hands.

Have notecards and pens available for rankings. To surprise fans of a particular brand, try offering it, plus several other beers in the same style, as part of a blind tasting. Cover each bottle up to the neck in aluminum foil, and tape a number to it. It's fun to keep people guessing as to the identity of the brew up to the end of the tasting, and it's easy to do.

# TABLESIDE TIPS

## CARE AND HANDLING OF BEER

Beer is a highly perishable product. Exposure to light and extreme temperatures can change flavors in a matter of minutes. At the Siebel Institute in Chicago, taste tests show there is a discernible difference in beer's flavor after just 15 minutes of exposure to direct sunlight. Even when protected from light and heat, beer ages and oxidizes more rapidly than does wine, with the exception of a few powerful brands. Most beers are best consumed within six months of bottling. Given the fragility of the flavors that brewers have worked so diligently to create, make sure to give beer proper care in storing and serving.

When purchasing beer, look for retailers who sell in volumes sufficient to rotate stock, keep their stock under refrigeration during storage, and display in only dimly-lit coolers. Avoid purchasing dusty bottles that have been out on open shelves, as time and warmer temperatures will stale beer more rapidly. Store your purchases in a refrigerator or a cool cellar (but do not let beer freeze). I often buy beer with a few friends: we purchase a closed case (checking its expiration or bottling dates first), split the costs and the beer, and take home the freshest possible six-packs.

Beer bottled with live yeast cells often fares better when stored in cool cellar conditions (45–55ºF). Be aware that some caps are improperly sealed: it is possible to get one bad-tasting bottle out of an otherwise fine quality six-pack, simply due to hidden oxidation and staling. Therefore, be willing to taste a beer on more than one occasion before passing final judgment, since so many chances exist for a beer to spoil, long before it reaches your glass. This is particularly true of beer that has been shipped to your locale from afar.

## POURING AND PRESENTATION

The correct pour for a bottle of beer depends on its condition and your taste. If the beer is bottled with live yeast, pour it carefully into a glass with sufficient room to accommodate the foam. Try tasting it without the yeast sediment, leaving the cloudy bits at the base of the bottle, and then taste it with the yeast. If the beer is highly carbonated, pour it into the center of the glass to give the lively carbonation a chance to settle before sipping. Some people enjoy the yeasty bite of an unfiltered hefe-weiss, so weiss beer glasses are extra tall to accommodate the spritzy collar of foam, beer, and sediments in a single pour.

How important is it to taste beer from a glass? Well, to enjoy a beer's color, carbonation, and full aromatics, it's necessary to pour the beer into a clear, clean glass. Appreciation of the luminous color, the size of the bubbles and collar of foam, and all the nuances of beer flavor are heightened by pouring and serving the beer in a glass, whether it is a pint glass or a curvaceous weiss beer glass.

Does the shape of the glass influence flavor perception? Anecdotal evidence leans toward more positive impressions of a beer that is served in its own uniquely designed glass. In fact, B. United Importers recently commissioned a special glass design for an eisbock, or ice beer, from the crystal glass makers Schott Zweisel. The glassware helps create a signature identity for the beer and makes an attractive presentation. Collectors of fine Belgian beers, such as Steve and Danielle Johnson of Le Belgique Gourmand, a true Belgian bistro in Virginia, also collect the stemware designed for each brand by the brewery. There are literally hundreds of styles of glassware, but most designs are based on aesthetic principles, not brewing science.

What beer glasses are most versatile? Britain's classic 20-ounce "pint" glass is a good choice for most beers, providing sufficient room for the contents of a 12- or 16-ounce bottle and its collar of foam. A shorter, flared and footed Brussels glass that holds 12 ounces suits most place settings. Pilsner and weiss beer glasses are gorgeous, but the larger ones can be tippy and are quite fragile. Snifters and glassware shaped like a thistle, the national symbol for Scotland, are tempting choices for barleywines and Scotch ales.

No matter what size or shape your glassware is, the most important factor is cleanliness. Glassware must be rinsed clean of soap, and dried without the dishwasher drying agents that can leave an odorous film on the surface. I rinse glasses twice: the first rinse water holds $\frac{1}{4}$ cup cider vinegar per gallon of hot water, the second is plain hot water. The vinegar helps cut any oily or soapy residue, and the final rinse takes away any smell of the vinegar. Dry glasses either by air drying or polishing with a lint-free cloth.

Temperature also influences the appreciation of beer. Avoid serving beer in frosty mugs: the icy cold glass will release water into the beer through condensation. Though many Americans are accustomed to drinking light lagers served very cold, more of the flavor and aroma of beer can be perceived at slightly warmer temperatures, as follows:

Light lagers 40–45°F
Fruit ales 40–50°F
Ales and dark lagers 45–55°F
Stouts, porters 50–55°F
Barleywines 50–60°F

Bert Grant recommended heating his spiced apple ale by popping a mug of it into the microwave, but most brewers shy away from warming beer. The heat destroys volatile hop aromas and carbonation, two of the elements most appreciated by beer drinkers.

# APPENDIX C
# TALK ABOUT TASTE

So many sources for tasting terminology exist, that this list is quite short compared to the beer dictionaries published by the Institute of Brewing Studies, International Association of Brewing Chemists, and other trade groups. But most drinkers just need to know a few terms to get started. Here are the basic definitions to help you describe the flavor sensations you perceive as you drink beer.

**APPEARANCE:** Look at the beer, holding it up to the light. If it looks cloudy, that may be due to yeast sediments or a protein haze from the malt. Examine the color, clarity, carbonation, and the "head" or foamy collar at the top of the glass. Bits of foam that cling to the sides of the glass are known as "Belgian lace." A glass with soap residue, or a plastic cup, may hinder the beer's foaming.

**BOUQUET:** What is the "nose" of the beer? Does the caramel or toasty aroma of the malt overpower the flowery or citrusy fragrance of the hops? Beer that is served too cold may lose aroma.

**FLAVOR:** When first sipping the beer, let it slide over your palate and remain on your tongue for a few seconds before swallowing. Look for characteristics such as dryness, nutty or caramel taste, sweetness, etc. See the terms below that people often use, or make up your own descriptors.

**BODY:** Is it creamy? Heavily carbonated and spritzy? Smooth and heavy? Try to identify the texture or mouthfeel.

**AFTERTASTE:** Beer usually has an aftertaste: a fresh flowery taste of hops, or an espresso-like or toffee taste; bready flavors of malted barley, or a pleasant bitterness. Beer that has a skunky aroma is light-struck. Beer that tastes like boiled cabbage is infected. Flavors that are rancid or oily indicate spoilage of the hops. Beer that is good and fresh will have a pleasant lingering maltiness or bitterness.

**DRINKABILITY:** The true test of a beer is whether you want to taste it again . . . and again . . . until the glass is empty!

APPENDIX D
# TERMINOLOGY

| BODY | TASTE | MOUTHFEEL |
|------|-------|-----------|
| full-bodied | flowery | dry finish |
| medium-bodied | fruity | grainy |
| balanced | coffee-like | creamy |
| strong | coppery | lively |
| intense | nutty | big/thick |
| flat | bitter | rich/sweet |
| softly malted | lemon | |
| sparkling | citric | **COLORS/CLARITY** |
| smooth | spice | opaque |
| complex | hoppy (bitter) | bright |
| silky | caramel | bead (carbonation) |
| crisp | toffee | luminous |
| thin | molasses | hazy |
| chewy | yeasty | cloudy |
| watery | cocoa or chocolatey | |

# APPENDIX E
# STYLE-FLAVOR-BRAND BEER GUIDE

The following list of styles and brands is organized by clustering styles by their dominant flavors and aromatics. Many styles of beer overlap in their flavor descriptors, so this list makes taste the unifying theme. The country or state of origin is indicated in parentheses behind the brand names. Contract brews are identified with their marketing headquarters, not the brewery location.

---

**STYLE(S):** Pale Ale
**AROMA & BOUQUET:** citrusy or fruity notes
**TASTE PROFILE:** highly hoppy; citric notes in North American versions; dry on the palate; moderate malt body
**BRANDS:** Bass, Double Diamond (UK); McAuslan St. Ambroise Pale Ale (CAN); Sierra Nevada Pale Ale (CA); Pyramid Pale Ale (OR); Gray's American Classic Pale Ale (WI); Summit Extra Pale Ale (MN); Tomcat Brewing Co. Cougar (NC)

---

**STYLE(S):** India Pale Ale, English and North American
**AROMA & BOUQUET:** flowery hop, with fruity notes; citric notes in North American version
**TASTE PROFILE:** strong to intensely bitter; dry; moderate malt body; long hoppy, dry finish; alcohol warming often evident
**BRANDS:** Anchor Liberty Ale (CA); Ballantine's Pale Ale (WI); Boulder Cliffhanger (CO); Brooklyn Brewing IPA (NY); Grants IPA (OR); Pike Brewing IPA (WA); Tremont Cask IPA (MA); Niagara Falls Gritstone Ale (CAN); Tomcat Brewing Co. Bengal IPA (NC)

---

**STYLE(S):** English and North American Brown Ale
**AROMA & BOUQUET:** flowery hop; subdued fruity notes
**TASTE PROFILE:** balanced; medium body; toasty malt
**BRANDS:** Samuel Smith's Nut Brown Ale, Newcastle Brown Ale (UK); Big Rock Warthog Ale (CAN); Brooklyn Brown Ale (NY); Oldenberg Brown Ale (KY); Pyramid Brown Ale (OR), Full Sail Brown Ale (OR); Sprecher Pub Brown Ale (WI); Yellow Rose Honcho Grande (TX)

**STYLE(S):** Best Bitter, North American Amber, German Altbier
**AROMA & BOUQUET:** hops and malt in balance; floral hops over soft malt notes; more floral or citric notes in North American versions due to domestically grown hops
**TASTE PROFILE:** full of character; robust malt; moderate to long finish
**BRANDS:** Fuller's London Pride, Young's Ramrod, Eldridge Pope Royal Oak, Shepherd Neame Spitfire (UK); Pinkus Müller Alt (GER); Shaftsbury Rain Forest Amber, Conners Best Bitter (CAN); Anderson Valley Boont Amber, Mad River Jamaica Red (CA); Deschutes Bachelor Bitter (OR); Old Thumper Extra Special Ale (ME); St. Arnold Amber (TX)

---

**STYLE(S):** Extra Strong Bitter (ESB)
**AROMA & BOUQUET:** hoppy; malt and ripe fruit clearly evident
**TASTE PROFILE:** robust hop and malt; hops bitterness balanced by residual malt sweetness; warming
**BRANDS:** Fuller's ESB, Bateman's Victory (UK); Sailor Hagar's Lohins ESB, Bowen Special Bitter (CAN); Redhook ESB (WA); Full Sail Equinox ESB (OR); Boulder ESB (CO); Rikenjaks ESB (LA); Miracle ESB (KS)

---

**STYLE(S):** Scottish or English Mild Ale (light and dark)
**AROMA & BOUQUET:** soft malty nose; little or no hop aromas
**TASTE PROFILE:** well-rounded; slightly malty; known as "session ales"
**BRANDS:** Bristol Brewing Laughing Lab Scottish Ale (CA); Left Hand Brewing Motherlode Golden Scottish Ale (CO); Grant's Scottish Ale (OR)

---

**STYLE(S):** Scottish Heavy Ale, Scottish Export Ale
**AROMA & BOUQUET:** huge malt; raisins, caramel, ripe fruit notes
**TASTE PROFILE:** malt sweetness; little or no hops apparent; medium body; warming
**BRANDS:** Belhaven St. Andrews, Caledonian Brewery MacAndrews (SCOT); Portland MacTarnahan's Ale (OR); Rikenjaks Hardhead Scottish Ale (LA)

**STYLE(S):** English Old (strong) Ale, Scotch Ale, North American Winter Warmers
**AROMA & BOUQUET:** clearly malty; some smoked aroma might be present in Scottish varieties; ripe fruit aromas in the ales
**TASTE PROFILE:** malty from start through finish; alcohol clearly evident; full body
**BRANDS:** Young's Old Nick, MacEwan's Scotch Ale (UK); Traquair House (SCOT); Deschutes Jubilale, Pyramid Snow Cap Ale, Full Sail Wassail Ale (OR); New Glarus Snowshoe Ale (WI); Samuel Adams Scotch Ale (MA); Odells 90-Shilling (CO); McNally's Extra Ale (CAN)

---

**STYLE(S):** Barleywines, Extra Strong Lagers
**AROMA & BOUQUET:** big malt, toasty; ripe fruit and other esters
**TASTE PROFILE:** strongly malty, almost syrupy; alcohol; full body
**BRANDS:** Eldridge Pope Thomas Hardy (yearly vintage) (UK); Samuel Adams Triple Bock (MA); Sierra Nevada Big Foot Barley Wine, Anchor Old Foghorn Barley Wine (CA); Rogue Old Crustacean, Hair of the Dog Adam Beer (OR)

---

**STYLE(S):** Robust or Brown Porter
**AROMA & BOUQUET:** roasted malt, hops, and fruity esters, all well-balanced
**TASTE PROFILE:** both hop and black malt bitterness; espresso notes; medium to full body; brown porters are slightly sweeter
**BRANDS:** Sierra Nevada Porter, Anchor Porter (CA); Chicago Brewing Big Shoulders Porter (IL); Redhook Blackhook Porter (WA); Great Lakes Edmund Fitzgerald Porter (OH); Woodstock Brewing Big Indian Porter (NY); Catamount Porter (VT); Summit Great Northern Porter (MN); Highland Brewing Co. Oatmeal Porter (NC); Spanish Peaks Porter (MT)

---

**STYLE(S):** Dark Lager, German Schwarz-Bier
**AROMA & BOUQUET:** low to medium hoppiness; malt notes, with fruity esters
**TASTE PROFILE:** malt or toasty, with low to medium hop bitterness; medium body
**BRANDS:** Kulmbacher Mönchshof Kloster Schwarz-Bier, Augustiner Dunkel Export (GER); Dixie Blackened Voodoo (LA); Thomas Kemper Bohemian Dunkel (WA); Sprecher Black Bavarian (WI); Sudwerk Hubsch Dunkel (CA); Weeping Radish (NC)

**STYLE(S):** Sweet (Milk or Cream) Stout
**AROMA & BOUQUET:** no hops apparent, but balance to maltiness of aroma
**TASTE PROFILE:** chocolate, caramel, roasted malt; medium to full body; warming
**BRANDS:** Samuel Adams Cream Stout (MA); Old Dominion Stout (VA); Whitbread Mackeson Stout (UK)

---

**STYLE(S):** Oatmeal Stout
**AROMA & BOUQUET:** some fruity esters; roast malt and chocolate notes
**TASTE PROFILE:** very smooth, malt and hops in balance; roasted malt, caramel, and chocolate notes on palate; alcohol warmth
**BRANDS:** Samuel Smith's Oatmeal Stout (UK); McAuslan St. Ambroise Oatmeal Stout (CAN); Anderson Valley Blarney Flats Oatmeal Stout (CA); New England Brewing Company Oatmeal Stout (MA); Rogue Shakespeare Stout (OR)

---

**STYLE(S):** Irish Dry Stout
**AROMA & BOUQUET:** coffee bean or burnt toast aromas
**TASTE PROFILE:** distinctive "roasty" notes, with hops to balance; medium to full body; long dry finish from hops, black malt, and roast barley
**BRANDS:** Guinness Stout, Murphy's Irish Stout (IR); Sierra Nevada Stout (CA); Shipyard Blue Fin Stout (ME); Coopers Stout, Sheaf Stout (Australia)

---

**STYLE(S):** Imperial Stout and Obsidian Stout
**AROMA & BOUQUET:** espresso roast
**TASTE PROFILE:** very dry; full body; thick, spirituous
**BRANDS:** Samuel Smith's Imperial Stout (UK); North Coast Old Rasputin Imperial Stout (CA); Steelhead Extra Stout (OR); New Glarus Coffee Stout (WI); Brooklyn Black Chocolate Stout (NY); Conners Imperial Stout, Wellington Co. Imperial Stout, Niagara Falls Extra Stout (CAN)

---

**STYLE(S):** Kölsch
**AROMA & BOUQUET:** soft floral notes
**TASTE PROFILE:** subtly sweet; good hop balance; light body
**BRANDS:** Küppers Kölsch (GER); Pyramid Kälsch (OR)

STYLE(S): Berliner Weissebier
AROMA & BOUQUET: fruity esters
TASTE PROFILE: acidic, from lactic acid; thin; very spritzy and carbonated
BRANDS: Berliner Kindl Weisse, Schultheiss Berliner Weisse, Haake-Beck Bremer Weisse (GER)

STYLE(S): Weizen/Weissbier (wheat-based)
AROMA & BOUQUET: cloves, vanilla, smoky, and fruity
TASTE PROFILE: highly carbonated; medium body; ripe banana; if unfiltered, yeasty tastes will be apparent
BRANDS: Spaten Fraziskaner Hefe-Weissebier, Schneider Weisse, Paulaner Hefe-Weizen (GER); Sprecher Hefe-Weiss (WI); Thomas Kemper Hefe-Weizen (WA); Chicago Brewing Heartland Weiss (IL); Tabernash Weiss (CO); August Schell Weizen (MN); Dogwood Brewing Co. Hefe-Weizen (GA)

STYLE(S): Dunkel (dark) Weizen, Weissbier or Weizenbock
AROMA & BOUQUET: malty, with fruity, chocolate, or clove notes
TASTE PROFILE: highly carbonated; malt sweetness; ripe fruit, roast malt, and chocolate notes; medium to full body
BRANDS: Erdinger Dunkel, Schneider Dunkel Weisse, Schneider Adventinus Dunkel Weizenbock (GER); Sprecher Brewing Co. Dunkel Weizen (WI)

STYLE(S): Tripel
AROMA & BOUQUET: well-rounded, rich combination of malt, ripe fruit, and yeasty notes
TASTE PROFILE: highly carbonated; ripe fruit; well-balanced; medium to full body; peppery alcohol notes
BRANDS: Affligem Tripel, Westmalle Tripel (BEL); La Trappe Tripel (NETH); New Belgium Trippel (CO); Hair of the Dog Golden Rose (OR)

STYLE(S): Belgian Wit (white or wheat)
AROMA & BOUQUET: spices, coriander, and orange peel; aroma hops
TASTE PROFILE: spicy, spritzy; some hop bitterness; some residual malt sweetness; thin to medium body
BRANDS: Hoegaarden Wit (BEL); Celis White (TX); Blue Moon Coors Wit, New Belgium Sunshine Wheat (CO); Thomas Kemper Belgian White (WA)

**STYLE(S):** Flanders Brown or Oud Bruin (Old Brown) Ale, Belgian Red Ale
**AROMA & BOUQUET:** roast malt and spicy notes; some lactic sourness, especially in the Belgian Red style
**TASTE PROFILE:** soft roast malt; tart; slight hoppiness; some spiciness; peppery alcohol notes
**BRANDS:** Gouden Carolus, Liefmans Goudenband, Rodenbach (BEL)

---

**STYLE(S):** Belgian Strong Ale
**AROMA & BOUQUET:** vinous notes over malt; some yeast odors
**TASTE PROFILE:** wine-like; earthy and straw notes; hoppy, medium body; alcohol warmth
**BRANDS:** Duvel, Hoegaarden Verboden Vrucht, Bush Scaldis, Kwak Pauwel (BEL); Unibroue Maudite (CAN); Celis Grand Cru (TX)

---

**STYLE(S):** Biére de Garde (North of France country ale)
**AROMA & BOUQUET:** hops aroma; earthy and straw notes
**TASTE PROFILE:** malty with very earthy, almost barnyardy notes; peppery alcohol
**BRANDS:** Duyck Jenlain, Jenlain Nöel, St. Sylvestre Trois Monts, La Choulette Sans Coulottes, Septante Cinq (France)

---

**STYLE(S):** Lambic, Gueuze Lambic
**AROMA & BOUQUET:** sour nose, cider
**TASTE PROFILE:** sour due to wild yeast fermentation; mild hops; thin body
**BRANDS:** Cantillon Lambic Grand Cru, Boon Gueuze, Lindemans Cuvée Rene (BEL)

---

**STYLE(S):** German Pilsner, Bohemian Pilsner
**AROMA & BOUQUET:** hoppy; slightly bready
**TASTE PROFILE:** assertively hoppy; malty; medium body
**BRANDS:** Pilsner Urquell (CR); Warsteiner Pils, König Pils (GER); Thomas Kemper Pilsner (WA); Stoudt Pilsener (PA); Saranac Golden (NY); August Schell Pils (MN); New Glarus Edel Pils (WI)

**STYLE(S):** Continental Pilsner, Continental Lager
**AROMA & BOUQUET:** some hoppiness
**TASTE PROFILE:** often brewed with corn, rice, wheat, or other adjuncts; somewhat hoppy; medium body
**BRANDS:** Heineken (NETH), Grolsch (NETH); Carlsberg Lager (DEN); Stella Artois (BEL); Becks (GER)

---

**STYLE(S):** Helles (light) Lager, Dortmunder Export
**AROMA & BOUQUET:** balanced malt and floral hops
**TASTE PROFILE:** malty; well-balanced; medium body
**BRANDS:** Paulaner, Spaten, DAB Export, Würzburger (GER); August Schell Export (MN); Great Lakes Dortmunder Gold (OH); Creemore Springs Lager (CAN)

---

**STYLE(S):** Märzen, Festbier
**AROMA & BOUQUET:** slightly bready
**TASTE PROFILE:** sweet malt; well-balanced; gently hopped
**BRANDS:** Stoudts Festbier (PA); Olde Heurich Maerzen (VA); Widmer (OR); Spaten Ur-Märzen, Hacker-Pschorr Märzen, Kulmbacher Mönchshof Märzen (GER)

---

**STYLE(S):** Vienna, Amber Lager
**AROMA & BOUQUET:** spicy hops
**TASTE PROFILE:** smooth malt, slightly tangy, crisp aftertaste
**BRANDS:** Abita Amber (LA); Thomas Kemper Amber Lager (WA); Great Lakes Eliot Ness Lager (OH); Tabernash Amber (CO); Anchor Steam Beer (CA); Upper Canada Rebellion Lager (CAN)

---

**STYLE(S):** Bocks, Maibocks, German (and Dutch and Belgian variants), Doppel Bocks
**AROMA & BOUQUET:** malty
**TASTE PROFILE:** malty, but with good hop balance; moderate hop bitterness; alcohol warmth
**BRANDS:** Ayinger Maibock, Spaten Franziskus Heller Bock, Paulaner Salvator, Ayinger Celebrator, EKU Kulminator 28 (GER); New Glarus Uff-da Bock (WI); Pyramid Bock (OR)

**STYLE(S):** North American Lager, Light Lager, Dry Lager, Cream Ale
**AROMA & BOUQUET:** light malt
**TASTE PROFILE:** crisp; slight hops bitterness; alcohol warmth in dry lager and cream ales
**BRANDS:** Budweiser, Miller, Coors Silver Bullet, Stroh Lager (US); Sleeman Cream Ale (CAN)

**STYLE(S):** North American Wheat Beer (may be lager or ale)
**AROMA & BOUQUET:** some fruity esters; malt not apparent
**TASTE PROFILE:** fruitiness; slight yeast bite; thin to medium body
**BRANDS:** Catamount Summer Wheat (VT); Stroh Augsburger Weiss (MN); Birmingham Brewing Red Mountain Wheat (AL); Widmer Hefe-weizen, Pyramid Wheaten Ale (OR); Golden Prairie Ginger Wheat (flavored with ginger) (IL)

**STYLE(S):** Belgian Fruited Beers and Fruited Lambics
**AROMA & BOUQUET:** fruity notes
**TASTE PROFILE:** well rounded, fruit flavors in balance with hops
**BRANDS:** Liefmans Frambozen, Lindemans Kriek, Boon Framboise, Rosé de Cantillon (BEL)

**STYLE(S):** North American Fruit Beers (lager, ale, some wheat beer-based)
**AROMA & BOUQUET:** varies according to presence of real fruit or extracts
**TASTE PROFILE:** some taste of real fruit, others taste medicinal (a cough drop in every bottle?)
**BRANDS:** Pete's Wicked Summer Ale (CA); Rogue 'n' Berry (marion berries), Pyramid Apricot Ale (OR); New Glarus Belgian Red Cherry Ale (WI); Niagara Falls Apple Ale (CAN); Samuel Adams Cherry Wheat (MA); Thomas Kemper Weizenberry (WA)

**STYLE(S):** Rauchbier (smoked)
**AROMA & BOUQUET:** wood-smoked malts, or "liquid smoke" which has an acrid, synthetic nose
**TASTE PROFILE:** smoky, malty
**BRANDS:** Rogue Smoke (OR); Dixie Smoke (LA); Zip City Rauchbier (NY); Kaiserdom Rauchbier, Aecht Schlenkerla (GER)

**STYLE(S):** Herb, Spice, and Vegetable Beers
**AROMA & BOUQUET:** varies by ingredients
**TASTE PROFILE:** varies with the ingredients used; careful balancing of malt and the extra ingredient(s) necessary; aging helps considerably in most instances
**BRANDS:** Woodstock Ichabod Crane (pumpkin & spices) (NY); Rogue Mexicali (chipotle pepper) (OR); Maclay Leann Fraoch (heather) (UK); Grant's Spiced Ale, Lakefront Pumpkin Lager (WA); Buffalo Bill's Pumpkin Ale, Bison Brewing Basil Honey Ale and Lemongrass Wheat (CA); Leinenkugel Honey Weiss (WI)

# INDEX